Vintage St. John

Discover St. John's History
Through Seven Generations of Heartfelt Stories

+200 Rare Photographs
of the
US Virgin Islands

Valerie Sims

A Family Memoir

7 Generations of

HEARTFELT STORIES

Shared within...

\+

The First Generation
with ties to St. John

The Second Generation

The Third Generation

Chapter 4

The Fourth Generation

Henry + 8 Children

Frank + 3 Children

Margie + 2 Children

The Fifth Generation

Chapter 8

Marion +5 children

Joan +4 children

Jackie +3 children

Diane + 2 Children

The Sixth Generation

Chapter 14

Leslie + 2 Children

The Seventh Generation

Vintage St. John

First Edition
ISBN: 978-1-7343863-0-1

Printed in the United States of America

Published by: Vintage World Media SEZC,
P.O. Box 32315, Grand Cayman, KY1-1209

Copyright Information

For Book Purchases

For more information visit, VintageVirginIslands.com and for book purchases, visit: VintageStJohnBook.com. Quantity books are available for educational use or as corporate gifts.

Author's Note

This book is a work of nonfiction. It is based on many interviews with the people who experienced the events told within as well as research in various archives, including out-of-print newspapers, personal diaries, and letters.

Memory and history are subjective, and any work of literary nonfiction has an element of subjectivity as well. I have done my best to adhere to the truth as my sources believe it to be throughout this book. The ideas and perspectives expressed within do not necessarily reflect the author's personal opinion.

Cover Photograph

The cover image is the author's grand uncle and aunt, Frank Creque, 12 years old and his sister, Margie Creque, 8 at Mary's Creek, St. John, US Virgin Islands, 1927.

A Free Gift to You

FREE bonus material is available for you as a gift to thank you for your purchase. It includes a video, family recipes, poems and more! Visit: VintageStJohnBook.com/bonus

Dedications

To my mother:
You are my biggest fan and fun companion on all my family history adventures! As you know, Mom, writing this book was a labor of love. Thank you for all your help and inspiration along the way.

To the descendants of Herman and Emily Creque:
Your ancestors loved their lands so much that they recorded the island's history for you through the photographs they took, the documents and letters they saved and the diaries they kept.

They left a wonderful legacy to treasure! Without their collections, this manuscript could never have been written.

This Book is for You Too ...

Virgin Islanders • Residents • Researchers • School teachers • Tour guides • Homeowners • Historians • Native St. Johnians • Visitors • Students • National Park Employees • Charter Captains • Real Estate Agents • School Librarians … and all those who contribute toward making St. John the special place it is today.

Additional Books by Family Members

Poems from a Small Island, Valerie Creque-Mawson

Persecuted and Prosecuted, Leon A. Mawson

Childhood Memories of Main Street, Marlene Mawson

STIGMA: Start to Imagine Giving More Acceptance, Leslie Carney

Island Boy Books, Arnold van Beverhoudt

Table of Contents

An Introduction .... *iii*
The Island of St. John, A Description .... *iv*

Chapter 1 Family Stories *1*
Chapter 2 A Life Lost ~ Leinster Bay, 1899 .... *13*
Chapter 3 Cultivating Cinnamon Bay, 1903 .... *49*
Chapter 4 Living at Lamesure Estate, 1922 .... *61*
Chapter 5 Purchasing Mary's Point Estate, 1927 .... *167*
Chapter 6 Acquiring Annaberg Estate, 1932 .... *179*
Chapter 7 Fun Times at Francis Bay, 1940s *197*
Chapter 8 Memories of Mary's Point, 1940s *233*
Chapter 9 The Virgin Islands National Park Idea, 1934 .... *241*
Chapter 10 Vacationing in Cruz Bay, 1955 .... *267*
Chapter 11 Finding Frank Bay, 1968 .... *277*
Chapter 12 Moving to Contant Enighed, 1979 .... *285*
Chapter 13 Casting off over Calabash Boom, 1982 .... *289*
Chapter 14 Remembering Caneel Bay, 1983 .... *299*
Chapter 15 The Seventh Generation *317*
Summary *318*

Notes .... *Lands the Creque Family Once Owned* *323*
Bibliography *332*
Acknowledgements *334*
About the Author *335*
Index *337*

Herman and Emily Creque

An Introduction

Vintage St. John is a collection of heartfelt stories handed down from generation to generation. They document a family's love affair with what was once a sparsely populated island in the Danish West Indies.

St. John offered observers a unique perspective unknown to flat, low-lying islands in the Caribbean—*the opportunity to admire a bird's eye view of a beautiful horizon.*

Long ago, an adventurous ancestor wanted to see this seascape for himself and trotted his way up through horse-worn trails to get to the highest crest. Within moments, a dazzling display of islands came into view.

By 1897, the estates of *Annaberg, Leinster Bay,* and *Abrams Fancy* became his and ever since, his lineage has shared a kinship with the island, leaving a memory bank of stories and memorabilia for their descendants.

Now, seven generations of memories reveal what life was like living, working, and vacationing near St. John's beautiful beaches and historic ruins.

St John was where the family felt most connected to nature, whether walking along white, sandy beaches, crisscrossing through Cruz Bay, or hang-gliding over tree-lined hilltops.

Beautiful beach vistas and panoramic landscapes instilled a sense of wonder at the island's natural beauty, the kind that made one marvel—not just at the remarkable scenery, but at life itself.

Interwoven throughout these stories are a few surprising gems.

Get ready to be transported back to a nostalgic time in St. John's history, when survival meant clearing the land for cattle pastures, cultivating the soil, and fishing—*all to feed one's family.*

Many of these narratives have been kept in the memories of distant ancestors while others were written in their diaries. They add to the cultural knowledge of several of the island's historic estates and are an important perspective in understanding St. John's rich history.

Raising livestock and overseeing the cultivation of bay leaves brought a sense of personal fulfillment for these ancestors because they contributed to the island's betterment as a whole.

Life was simpler in the olden days with simple pleasures, but there were also times of hard, physical labor, personal loss and untold suffering.

For the younger generation, it was a carefree time of innocence, a playful time of curiosity and discovery—*until the unthinkable happened.*

St. John has changed considerably since the late nineteenth century, but many of the island's captivating charms have not. Crystal-clear, aquamarine waters still offer the most refreshing swims, while beautiful, bursting sunsets signal the end of another miraculous day.

Thank you for your interest in St. John's past.

You're sure to have a new reverence and appreciation for the struggles and resiliency of those who paved the way from yesteryear to this year.

Vintage St. John
N
W
E
S
Mary's Point
Leinster Bay
Francis Bay
Cinnamon Bay
Trunk Bay
Annaberg Estate
Abrams Fancy
Caneel Bay
East End
Coral Bay
Ferry Dock
Cruz Bay
Friis Bay
Estate Contant Enighed
Lamesure Estate
Calabash Boom
Frank Bay
Star Villas
Genti Bay
Ditliff Pt
Ram's Head
©VSims

The Island of St. John

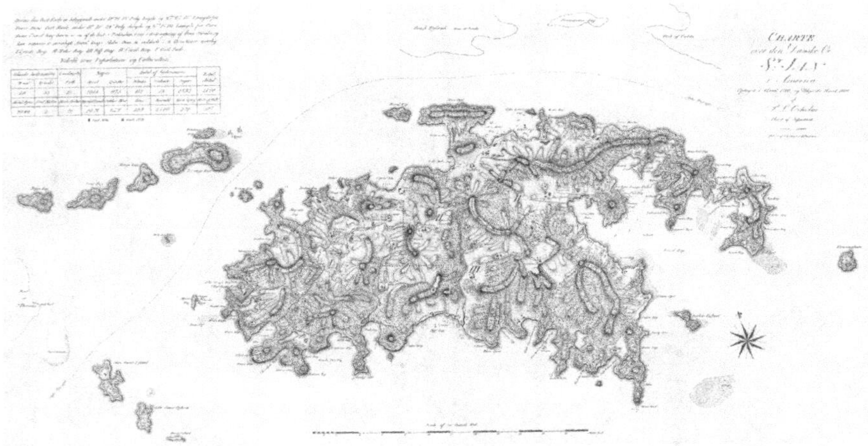

A map of St. Jan, Danish West Indies, P.L. Oxholm, 1780 © The Royal Library of Denmark

A Description

The little island of St. John is one of a special group of islands making up the US Virgin Islands, nestled in the vibrant, blue waters of the West Indies. Its area is about twenty square miles, nine miles long and five miles wide, roughly the size of the island of Manhattan in New York.

When visitors first discovered this rugged and mountainous isle with its coastline of powdery beaches, it became a place of rest and relaxation for those looking for a haven in a tropical setting.

Once under the Danish flag, it was ceded to the United States in 1917, along with the main islands of St. Thomas, St. Croix, and countless smaller islands nearby.

Since then, it has been a part of America's dominion, but it still holds onto a few Danish customs, including its street names and left-hand driving.

Christopher Columbus named these islands, *Las Once Mil Virgenes,* in honor of a young girl and her maidens, martyred for their Christian beliefs of sanctity.

Although he did so, he never came ashore on St. John when he sailed through the islands in November 1493. Since his visit, countless others have and were profoundly struck by the island's natural beauty.

According to a writer with the *New York Herald-Tribune,* the views from the heights of St. John are lovely.

Every new summit brings its fresh arrangement of bold headlands, white beaches, blue water above coral reefs, and a sea so clear that as the big cumulus clouds roll slowly overhead, one can see their shadows traveling across the bottom.

The swimming is nothing short of heavenly—crystal clear water, white-sand beaches and little reef-protected bays so translucent, that in 1931, Arthur Ruhl said of it, 'in a small boat, you seem suspended in the air.'

Chapter 1

Family Stories

Aimee Linda de Lagarde

A Quest to Find the Truth

Have you ever been told a family story that you thought was just too outlandish to be true? Did you try to research it further?

As a family historian, I've been listening and jotting down the most incredible stories ever since I was a young girl.

On a quest to find the truth, I met a distant relative who offered to help me figure out facts from fiction. Little did I know that it would be the beginning of a journey through seven generations of St. John's history!

Aimee's Story

Aimee de Lagarde was just as enthusiastic about genealogy as I was. I met her for the first time in St. Thomas in 2009, after learning that we shared the same charismatic ancestor.

Louis Eugène de Lagarde was Aimee's grandfather and the author's third, great-grandfather. He was born on the island of St. Thomas in 1835, under the Danish flag.

Aimee never knew him, but her father spoke to her often about her family's history, telling her all about the de Lagarde's first arrival in the islands and their reasons for immigrating there.

Although Harry de Lagarde passed away in 1958, she never forgot those family stories, and I was grateful because Aimee promised to impart some of what she learned to my mother, Marlene and me.

My mom and I were beyond thrilled! Finally, someone with the missing pieces of our past that would be able to answer many of my burning questions.

I'd been researching for years and had been waiting for this day for a long time. When we met at a restaurant in Crown Bay, I knew I was only moments away from discovering a few family secrets.

With pen and paper in hand, I jotted down the stories Aimee shared as fast as I could. Here are the tantalizing tales she told us of murder and mystery, some believable—and some out of this world!

You can decide for yourself… facts, or fiction?

Count de Lagarde's Untimely End

Stories the family passed down from generation to generation became more and more intriguing as time went by. Aimee spoke of an ancestor known simply as Count de Lagarde, whose son emigrated to the Danish West Indies at a time when his father was under suspicion for treason in France.

One version of the story that never changed was the murder of this notorious Count, a member of a privileged social class during the Middle Ages.

It was said that he met a grisly end at the guillotine.

A Tale of Treason

The author, J. Antonio Jarvis shared a brief story about the family in his book, *The Virgin Islands and Their People.*

He reported that:

'The family emigrated to the Danish West Indies after Pierre de Lagarde, their progenitor, was executed for treason. They were originally French minor nobility from Normandy who could trace their history back to the time of Christopher Columbus.'

Studies have shown that seventy-eight percent of the executions by guillotine during this time were for treason and rebellion. Ten percent were for federalism, a term that meant resisting further revolutionary changes and nine percent were for holding questionable opinions.

The latter point alone makes me grateful I am not living in that period; how many of us can honestly say we don't hold a few questionable opinions—at least, as others may see it!

The details of the Count's offending crime are not known, but he and his wife both reportedly suffered the same unspeakable fate.

Unbelievably, the guillotine was proposed as a more humane method of execution since beheadings by the sword or ax were often botched, and several attempts would be needed before the victim succumbed to his fate.

As my mother and I sat at the table with Aimee, we listened quietly with great anticipation. The de Lagardes' were distant relatives and we were filled with both shock and curiosity.

The Family Album

From old photographs found in their family albums and oral stories passed down, Count de Lagarde was described as having a small body frame, red hair, and wide, Victorian sideburns that graced his jawline. According to one of his descendants, an image once existed of him dressed in full military regalia, including his sword and epaulets with several medallions attached to his breast.

Unfortunately, the family album has disappeared.

Fleeing to the West Indies

Aimee told us that months before the Count's untimely death, he arranged to send his children to the French West Indies for safety.

When they boarded a steamer for their long journey, port authorities were told the governess was the children's mother. In her care were two of his sons and a daughter, dressed to appear unkempt and slovenly.

Woven into the hem of her petticoat were precious family heirlooms and around her midsection, stuffed tightly into her corset, were small bags of gold and silver currency. They protruded to such a degree that it gave her the appearance of an expectant mother.

In her luggage were three trunks of gold!

Although fanciful and most certainly embellished over the years, this part of the story had us captivated.

The Steamer Stops in St. Thomas

At some point during the steamer's long passage, the Governess became critically ill, and when the ship anchored in the harbor of Charlotte Amalia, she was taken to the hospital.

Members of the Church's congregation looked after the children until she recovered. When she did, she purchased a beautiful property overlooking Charlotte Amalie, known as *Harbor View Estate.*

On the deed, she reportedly signed the name, *de Lagarde,* raised the children as her own, and never returned to France. The reason she decided to stay, Aimee said, was because *'she was treated so kindly by everyone she encountered.'*

Romain de Lagarde ~ 1832

While researching further to verify Aimee's story, I discovered that in 1832, a direct relation with the name of *Romain de Lagarde* immigrated to St. Thomas with the intention to settle and practice his art as a patented architect.

On the contrary, he was not a child traveling with a governess and siblings, but as an adult accompanied by a large family of his own. This was very different from the story Aimee shared about how the de Lagarde's first arrived in St. Thomas.

Sadly, Aimee passed away in 2011, and I'm unable to share this recent discovery with her. She would have been surprised to learn of this twist. Perhaps further research will shed light on the governess and how she came to play a role in her father's story.

The Count of No Account

Romain was baptized *Joseph Felix de Catalina Romain Lagarde de Alacuas et Montes de Oca*. It was said that he inherited the title of Count but was known simply as *Romain de Lagarde.*

In the Danish Islands, the title held little value, and because of this, his family lovingly referred to him as *The Count of No Account.* According to the newspapers, he was simply, R. Lagarde and sometimes, just *Lagarde.*

The Gift of Poetry

Shortly after Romain settled, he announced to the public that he carried *'a very detailed certificate, issued by a General of Genius, under the orders of which he worked for more than twelve consecutive years.'*

In addition to his love of architecture, he had a gift for poetry and shared his poems and religious prayers in the newspaper. Written in the form of fables and vignettes, they were always in another language other than English.

Romain had an aptitude for the easy command of both the French and Spanish languages and wrote about the events that impacted his life.

The Hurricane of 1837 that devastated St. Thomas and the passing of the Great Comet of 1843 were two of the most noteworthy. Many residents were afraid and believed the comet traveled so low in the sky that it would skim over their heads. Others believed it was a sign the world was coming to an end.

Although it passed relatively close to the surface of the sun, Romain wrote a heartfelt poem to allay everyone's fears, reassuring them that it was still many miles away.

Sketching Building Plans ~ 1833

With years of experience sketching building plans, Romain was ahead of his time and his talents considered innovative for the nineteenth century.

His drawings included detailed cuts and elevations so his clients could see the exact buildings, both internally and externally, before they were built.

He and his family were residents at the Union Hotel of Madame Veuve Cayol.

This was located at #16 Church Street, situated in Christiansted, St. Croix, until they found themselves a permanent residence.

A Business Partnership

Within a few months, Romain formed a business relationship with a colleague he met on the island. He and Jean Peyredieu designed private homes, temples, and public buildings together.

With a reputation for distinction, they put the '*greatest burden upon their work, both in terms of elegance and durability.*' According to an advertisement in *The Sanct Thomae Tidende* newspaper, the partners held one infallible secret they hoped would make them a success. It was a system that would *'prevent the wood from becoming rotten in masonry and concrete.'*

It's uncertain whether this venture was successful for the two, but they did make a significant effort to advertise their services.

Opening a Private School ~ 1840

Eight years after arriving on the island, Romain took an interest in opening a private school in the heart of Charlotte Amalie with one of his sons.

He *'received a moderate number of select scholars, in the education of whom he dedicated himself, with all the affection of a good father to beloved children.'*

Two years later—in August 1842, two of his daughters arrived from France to assist Romain at the school. The eldest was about twenty years of age and received an education under the *'most careful of guidance.'*

This enabled her to *'instruct and bring up young ladies in a satisfactory manner to their parents, who placed their children under her tuition.'*

For three dollars per month, she taught French, arithmetic, history, and geography, and for an additional dollar, sewing and embroidery were included for the girls.

Situated on a nearby hilltop, the school had a beautiful view of the harbor with its cluster of trading ships anchored below.

Charlotte Amalie harbor, St. Thomas, Danish West Indies © The Royal Library of Denmark

Romain was the schoolmaster and presided over both schools, keeping the school for boys separated from the girls. He made sure that *'the strictest attention and decorum were observed in the classes.'*

Romain's Relatives

The de Lagardes' had several children: Alberic; Caroline; Eleonor; and Juste to name a few, all born in France during the 1820s.

While living in St Thomas, Romain and Louise Eugenie Miquelles welcomed a son on December 13, 1835. His name was Louis Eugène de Lagarde.

Eugène became the author's first direct ancestor with ties to St. John.

Not much more is known about Romain and his wife.

At a point in time, they wished to leave the island and considered either selling or renting their home. However, there was an entry in the St. Thomas Death Registry for Louise, who was originally from Haiti. It recorded her death on the island on July 11, 1875, at seventy-six years of age.

Eugène remained in St. Thomas.

Approximately one dozen gold medals and epaulets and at least two dozen gilded scabbards with ribbons were gifted to him. They were all that was left of his ancestor's prized possessions from France. His great-grandchildren played with them from time to time, otherwise, he rarely spoke of his family's past.

THE *First* GENERATION

Louis Eugène de Lagarde

Owner of Estates Annaberg • Abrams Fancy • Leinster Bay

Chapter 2

A Life Lost ~ Leinster Bay ~ 1899

Louis Eugène de Lagarde was very likely named for the French King, *Louis the Great*, a powerful monarch who reigned during the seventeenth century.

The name Louis, meant *renowned warrior*, and combined with the masculine name Eugène, which meant *noble* and *well-born*, Eugène was destined to leave his mark in the world.

He was a bright, intellectual boy and when he was twelve, his father placed a notice in the Tidende newspaper for him for a job as a clerk.

'He reads and writes with facility, the English, Spanish and French languages,' the paper reported on March 8, 1848. Indeed, Eugène was well-versed in both English and French literature.

He had the advantage of reading Lord Chesterfield, Victor Hugo, François de La Rochefoucauld, Alfred de Musset, Alphonse de Lamartine, and occasionally looked over the works of Voltaire.

His understanding of French culture from the writings of these influential poets and politicians helped frame many of his opinions during his lifetime. He relied on them extensively when he wrote to the newspaper or debated with learned men at council meetings.

Emancipation ~ 1848

Four months after Eugène found part-time employment, slavery in the islands was abolished.

'*All unfree in the Danish West India Islands are from today, emancipated,'* wrote the Governor, Peter Carl Frederik von Scholten on July 3, 1848. Denmark approved the sanction so that in the future, no bondage shall ever exist for any part of the population of their West India Islands.

Eugène was coming of age, turning thirteen later that year. Having studied the great authors and thinkers of his time, he knew more about the perils of slavery than most of his contemporaries. Like Mazzini, he believed that '*God's laws commanded men to love and serve each other as brethren.'*

Lord Chesterfield, a society figure, whose writings Eugène respected, believed *'every human creature had a right to liberty which cannot be taken from him unless he forfeited it by some crime.'*

Unfortunately, Eugène's father felt differently. Perhaps the influence of his upbringing during the eighteenth century was the reason why he felt servitude was an allowable practice.

When in 1842, a Mulatto woman named Celestine, absconded from his residence, he was angrier with the person who persuaded her to leave, than he was with her, offering to pay double to discover who it was.

He didn't believe she would leave on her own accord. One doubloon was offered as a reward for anyone who would apprehend her and two doubloons to anyone who could prove to the Police Court that she had been *'persuaded to absent herself from his service.*

Consul General of Haiti

According to the author, J. Antonio Jarvis, the family first arrived in St. Thomas as *Consul General of Haiti*, representing the Haitian government at a time when the island was the great trading center of the Caribbean. Indeed, Eugène once held this title, a position his father may have held as well.

Although born in St. Thomas, he had strong ties to Haiti since his mother's family was from the island. With his '*unremitting zeal and exertion in all questions relating to the welfare of his native isle,'* he was a natural candidate to fill the position.

Eugène traveled to Port-au-Prince often as the official representative acting on behalf of Haitian citizens living in the Danish West Indies. He also facilitated trade and friendship between the people of the two countries.

The Haitian dispatch boat, *Toussaint L'Ouverture* © Histarmar.com.ar

It was his duty to keep the French community of St. Thomas informed on newsworthy matters, which he did by reprinting telegraphic dispatches he received from the Haitian President, Florvil Hyppolite.

Sometimes, the Haitian gunboat, *Toussaint L'Ouverture,* paid a visit to St. Thomas directly, delivering dispatches and news to Eugène from Port-au-Prince.

Everyone knew when Eugène went aboard because gun salutes were exchanged with the Fort Christian Battery as he disembarked, sending puffs of smoke clouds into the air.

A Colorful Character

As an adult, Eugène was a colorful character, a true ladies' man of his day. Confident and charismatic, his indiscretions with women had acquaintances in St. Thomas gossiping about him, especially about the nine children he had between his three marriages and as many as nine illegitimate children outside his marriages.

His infidelities angered and hurt his family, with some members calling him *'a reprobate,'* and others calling him, *'a dirty rat!'* Disparaging remarks circulated throughout the town that he likely fathered *all* of the offspring born on Frenchman's Hill and at least one in every island that he visited.

Neighbors and family members may have been partially right; Eugène was a common ancestor on Marlene's side of the family, both on her mother's side and her father's side.

Despite all the innuendos, he was a brilliant businessman and dedicated himself to the affairs of his country before his own. He began his career as a writing clerk in 1862 when his first son was born, then became Chief Clerk at the British Postal Agency in 1864.

That year, thousands of Danish countrymen were killed and captured fighting in the Second Schleswig War in Denmark. This had a negative impact on St. Thomas because of its close political and economic relationship with Denmark. Eugène politely reminded his creole friends how important it was to *'fulfill their patriotic duty'* by contributing to the relief fund for the victims' relatives. Many who nobly fell had been defending their mother country under overwhelming odds.

A Colonial Council Member ~ 1866

By 1866, Eugène had been elected to the Colonial Council to represent the Town of St. Thomas with twenty-three votes out of a total of fifty-nine. He was outspoken at times during the Council meetings, especially when the new government house was being built and decorated.

Because some of the constituents considered the finished building to be *'excessively ugly and to suffer other deficiencies'*, a proposal was suggested for the granting of $500 for decorations. Eugène felt that the work should be put up for bid, and artists could come from as far away as Martinique and other places to finish the job.

The Cholera Epidemic Returns ~ 1866

There were more serious matters to address though, as the infectious disease of cholera was threatening the islands again. All the houses and dwellings had to be whitewashed inside and out.

Any case of sudden or suspicious illness was reported immediately to the authorities so that the infected could be isolated and taken to the hospital.

During earlier years, from December 24, 1853, to February 4, 1854, there were 1,116 deaths from this infectious malady. It was a very difficult time in the history of the islands.

On St. John, for instance, the highest death toll during the month of January 1854, took place at Cinnamon Bay where the disease claimed the lives of 142 people.

A year after cholera returned to claim more victims, another calamity struck the islands that sent terror into the hearts of the innocent. It arrived on a lovely November afternoon, as many lay down for an afternoon nap after lunch.

The aftermath of the Hurricane of 1867 in St. Thomas © Illustrated London News

A Hurricane, Earthquake and Tidal Wave Cause Death and Destruction ~ 1867

'On the morning of November 18, the sun rose as bright and as beautiful as ever it did. The birds sang their morning hymns as usual; men went forth to their businesses, and all nature reposed in its usual security.

No one expected that God, on that fateful day, was going to manifest his Almighty Power.' ~ T.M. Krause

At about ten minutes to three p.m., Eugène was probably relaxing in his parlor when suddenly, the vibration of the earth commenced instantaneously and so violently that he and his family could barely make their way outside.

There they stood for some time as the ground oscillated at a fearful rate, so much so that hundreds of people around them were on their knees, imploring the very mercy of heaven. Eugène tried to protect his children as much as he could, thinking it would soon be over when suddenly, there was an awful shriek! The sea had receded and was coming in! They immediately hastened to the highest eminence from which they beheld the second roll of the sea. The seemingly twenty-foot-high wall of water, with its snowy whiteness, was coming for all of them!

Feelings of the Times

A Poem by T.M. Krause

When we wake in the morning, who can tell,
Ere night might be tolled our funeral bell.
Old earth tremble, with great convulsive shakes,
Holding the power of the dread earthquakes.

Oh, who can surmise how long she may last,
When six thousand years of trouble have passed.
The evening of time is closing around,
But man does not like to be told that sound.

Christians be brave, why need you fear at all?
The earth may be crushed, but you cannot fall.
He that keeps Israel never will sleep,
And your interest safe, He ever will keep.

"Sadly, the islands' legacy is one of earthquakes, conflagrations, revolts, gales, and diseases, all calamities not to be effaced from the tablet of memory, even by *the destructive finger of time."*

An Agent for The St. Croix Avis ~ 1867

Shaken by this life-changing event, Eugène was happy to be alive. He had lost all his possessions, but not his perspective.

Later that same year, he became an agent for *The St. Croix Avis* newspaper while living in St. Thomas. This was advantageous for him because he wrote about matters concerning him the most, hoping to have an impact on influencing them for the better.

A few years later, he was re-elected to the Colonial Council, but this time, he represented the island of St. John. ~ *1871 to 1874*

Arguments Against Boys Sent to St. John ~ 1873

There was one pending matter above all else concerning St. John that Eugène felt strongly about. When he discussed it with His Excellency, it sparked a heated debate among the Councilmen when several members took opposing perspectives.

Eugène was concerned about the practice of sending *young, idle boys,* found on the streets of St. Thomas to work on St. John '*weeding canes and minding cattle.*'

As the *First Member for St. John*, he asked his constituents:

"Why are little children, natives of St. Thomas, that are taken up in the streets by the police, exiled to the islands of St. John and St. Croix?

Whether it is by the Government's authority that these cruel acts are committed by the police, and, if so, whether they can be considered to suit the time and age of liberty in which we live.

Instances of this practice by police, to send little children found idling in the streets away to St. John are becoming too frequent."

Eugène was surprised that such a thing could be done in their *'enlightened community.'* Only a few days ago, he said, three little boys had been sent in this manner to St. John. What crime, then, had these children committed?

Banished to Weed Canes and Mind Cattle

He had no idea, but said they were banished, not even legally so—with at least the freedom to choose their place of banishment—but sent off like chattels to some plantation on St. John, *'to weed canes and mind cattle on a diet of sour cornmeal and rotten herrings.'*

He pleaded with the Government to take the matter in hand and do the rightful thing and return the children.

A young boy on St. John, Danish West Indies © The Royal Library of Denmark

How long were these unfortunates thus bound? Eugène was unable to say, but it may be presumed that they were obliged to serve until their twenty-fifth year, which according to Danish law was the age of majority.

But this is surely a great wrong, Eugène argued, and it is not to be tolerated at any time when *'liberty is the inheritance of all.'*

And what becomes of the children thus torn away from the bosoms of their parents? If they can live through the privations of their exile, they cannot escape the taint of the associations into which they have been forced. They will grow up to be fit for nothing but the jail, and the convict-gang, being taken away from their place of birth and from their friends and relations, to work on a plantation amongst criminals and drunkards. Dire consequences are inevitable!

Eugène was not opposed to the public finding occupation for those who had no work, but he was opposed to the idea of '*sending children into misery for the sake of supplying St. Croix or St. John with cheap labor.*'

Paying off the Police

There was a questionable report circulating that as much as sixteen dollars had been given to certain parties in the police force for a boy or a laborer sent to St. John in this manner. In some instances, parents of the children had consented to the banishment of their offspring.
Eugène reminded his associates of a proverb:

"There are many ways of killing a dog besides choking him, and in the same manner, there are many other ways to establish slavery in these islands than openly proclaiming it."
He went on to say:

"The banishment of children to St. Croix or St. John is a step in that direction of slavery... Against slavery, I protest, and in the name of equity and humanity, I demand that the exiled children be sent back."

Other speakers believed the islands benefited from this measure, which took vagrants away from the streets and found work for them on St. John. Many thought it was good for the boys.

Children of the Danish West Indies © The Maritime Museum of Denmark

Boys Better Off

They must work, but they are better provided for, better fed, in short, better off, where they are now than in the place and surroundings from where they were taken.

They would certainly have a greater chance of becoming fit for the convict-gang, than by growing up on St. John as honest laborers. If the boys sent there were under thirteen years of age, the owner of the estate must send them to school and was responsible for their proper attendance. It was clear that the boys were, in fact, better off on the estate than in the streets: *'St. John got laborers and St. Thomas got rid of vagrants.'*

An example was shared of a man who in St. Thomas was a well-known vagrant and nuisance, but who was on St. John, a quiet, steady laborer.

Others argued that it was not an act of cruelty, but humanity, to put young vagrants to honest work instead of leaving them to *'prowl about at will.'*

"It must not be forgotten that the police have caught such mischievous boys in the act of setting fire to a lumber yard. It is beyond a doubt that when in service on St. John, the children are better off learning to work."

Eugène maintained his position, reminding everyone that the children last sent to St. John in this manner had not committed any crime. *'They were taken up while playing marbles in the street.'*

The Illegal Sale of Lottery Tickets

The 3rd Member for St. Thomas, Mr. Richardson, was against one of the activities the vagrant children engaged in, which he believed was responsible for their situation.

"It is a fact," he said, *"that the illegal sale of lottery tickets is the means of inducing many youths to vagrancy. We are every day pestered by boys running about selling these tickets. If the police would catch these boys and send them off to honest work on St. John as fast as they were caught, it would benefit this community and the boys too."*

Eugène said that in doing so, we would act unjustly. The children who sold the tickets were not the real offenders—they didn't buy the tickets for sale; they were ordered by their parents or employers to sell the tickets and if they didn't do it, they would get a thrashing.

If we must banish somebody to St. John, Eugène insisted, then we should banish those unnatural parents that made those children vagrants and afterward beg the police to exile them.

Eugène said the unnatural parents that could desire or even permit their offspring to be driven away in this manner, must surely be born under the regime of the whip.

Others argued back that the children were sent to the Judge on St. John who placed the children in good service to the community.

When his Excellency finally read a section of the Vagrant law, it proved that the policemen were warranted in finding employment for *'idle and unprotected children.'*

No Doctor for St. John ~ 1873

A few weeks later, Eugène learned the Communal Physician was ill and not able to attend to patients on St. John.

He inquired at the following Council meeting whether any physician had been directed to the island during Dr. Brondsted's illness, concerned that the island was left without a doctor.

According to the statutes, a medical doctor must visit the island once every month, alternately between Cruz Bay and Carolina or another suitable place in the East End.

First Crown Member, Dr. Magens, said voluntary assistance was rendered by other physicians, but no physician had been sent to St. John since no one was aware there was a need for help there.

The Second member for St. John, Mr. McDonald, did not think the matter was said correctly, *'that there were no sick people on St. John in need of help.'*

The fact was, *'there are sick people, but those confined to bed cannot get near the doctor when he comes, as his visits are too short.'*

The physician had, as far as the speaker knew, made one trip to Coral Bay about two months ago.

Dr. Brondsted
© The Royal Library of Denmark

'But good heavens,' Eugène said. *'What has become of our principals that we neglect the people in their time of need?* He was incensed by their lack of good judgment.

Dr. Magens explained that notice was given of the doctor's arrival in plenty of time for those able to come to him and also for those unable to call personally, to send to him, in which case he would go to the patient. Since no such application was made, the doctor could not know that his services were required.

The Governor stepped in before the matter became heated, to say he did not think it right for members of the Council to bring forward public complaints against the municipal officers without any previous notice.

It had to be remembered, the governor said, that the men thus complained of could not defend themselves, nor could government, whose duty it was to see that the public officers properly discharged their functions. His Excellency would only say that no complaint of the Communal Physician's manner of discharging his duty had ever been made to the government.

Eugène knew that St. John could not afford to pay a physician on its own at $1,000 annually and needed assistance from St. Thomas.

He defended his position by saying he never intended to bring any complaint against the physician, he had simply, for the sake of information, inquired whether any arrangement had been made to replace him during his illness. The matter was soon dropped, and no-one offered another word.

Dedicated to his Duties

Eugène viewed his position as a public servant with strong authority.

He considered every official ought, *"without a doubt, sacrifice his leisure hours and holidays... to the service of the state, without any extra payment, to perform the duties he had undertaken to do.*

"Some would-be aristocrats of this place," he said, *"would certainly denounce me as being too punctilious for the island's good, because sometimes I advocated things for its benefit, contrary to other's interest.*

"I shall continue to expose what I consider to be a wrong done to the community of my dear native land. Some folks, who are not personally acquainted with me, may probably suppose me to be vindictive, but no. What I am doing, I consider a right, and therefore I will maintain my point."

Rue St-Denis after the fire, Martinique, 1890 © The Caribbean Photo Archive

Charitable Contributions ~ 1890

When a fire destroyed the central town of Martinique, Eugène was one of the first patrons to donate to the relief fund. He cared for his fellow countrymen, both at home and afar.

Although it was only five dollars, in those days, that was quite a substantial sum. This fire was a devastating disaster that destroyed 1600 dwellings, obliterating three-quarters of the town. It left hundreds of families homeless.

Many worldwide disasters revealed the charitable nature of those living and visiting the Danish West Indies. Subscription lists filled the newspapers with the names of those who gave so willingly. From twenty cents to $200, many contributed what they could.

Even the captains and crews from the vessels anchored in the harbor collected funds to help the unfortunate and there were many calamities both in the islands and abroad.

The steamship *RMS Amazon* on fire, 1852 © Illustrated London News

Not only did the island collect for its own inhabitants after the cholera epidemic in 1854, the St. Croix Labor Riot of 1878, and the Hurricane of 1899, but it also collected for those far away, like the famine in Iceland in 1882, the volcanic eruption in Martinique in 1902, and the families of the lost on the steamship, *RMS Amazon*, in 1852. The ship blazed out of control on its maiden voyage to the West Indies and sent 100 souls to a watery grave.

Other countries reciprocated and sent funds to help the Danish West Indies during its time of need. Considerable resources were raised in Denmark for those ravished by the Hurricane of 1871 and those displaced by the fire that destroyed Christiansted in 1880. Small islands like St. Barthelemy, with very little to give themselves, offered up *'prayers to heaven to arrest the progress of cholera'* when it returned to St. Thomas again.

Despite the relatively small size of the Danish West Indies and its distant location from the continents of ruling nations, the newspapers kept the community abreast of worldwide events. Everyone helped each other when they could with money, clothes, food, medicines, provisions or with prayers.

Three St. John Estates for Sale ~ 1895

In early 1895, *The Tidende* newspaper announced the impending sale of three St. John properties belonging to the estate of an esteemed gentleman, Antoine Anduze. This was of interest to Eugène because Anduze's properties were all prime estates, including *Annaberg Estate*, *Abrams Fancy,* and *Leinster Bay* on the island's north-west side.

Mr. Anduze was a partner in a retail establishment selling a general assortment of merchandise, including everything from hardware, glassware, and china, to pale ale, champagne, and wines by the case. He was one of the largest land proprietors in the islands when he passed away at the age of sixty-seven on July 10, 1892.

Eugène knew of St. John's beauty and considered making such a purchase. After all, St. John produced the largest and best fruits, including bananas, limes, lemons, pineapples, guavas, and oranges. However, a hurricane had passed through several years prior and destroyed many of the crops, including thousands of banana trees, leaving the island virtually decimated.

As one of the island's previously-elected representatives, he remained cautious about making a hasty decision. Consumed by pressing matters, he spent a significant time attending business meetings, traveling, and spending time with his large family in St. Thomas

.

According to research conducted by David W. Knight, Sr., during the nineteenth century, it was common for St. Thomas businessmen to own vast acres of land on St. John for farming and raising livestock. They were absentee owners for the most part but traveled back and forth to monitor their estate's progress and development.

It's possible, the arrival of a Danish royal to St. John may have been the impetus Eugène needed to move forward.

The Royal Visit of HRH Prince Carl ~ 1896

In January, a visit from His Royal Highness, Prince Carl, brought the two towns of Coral Bay and Cruz Bay together to plan the largest welcoming party the island had ever seen!

Prince Carl was serving as a Second Lieutenant aboard the Danish Cruiser, *Fyen,* sailing through the West Indies with a complement of 300 men and officers. The *Fyen* was a huge frigate, 220 feet long, forty-five feet broad, protected by a battery of eighteen large and seven small guns.

As she sailed into view, the Danish National flag was hoisted at Christiansfort, a sign to all of the ship's approach. Suddenly, the heavy anchor splashed down as hundreds of feet of heavy chain followed, rattling and echoing across the harbor when she settled into her position near Steven's Cay.

A gun salute of fifteen booming cannons announced the Prince's impending arrival. Billows of smoke in the air could be seen for miles before they floated away in the breeze.

Everyone knew the royal visitor was soon on his way! At the dock, a huge red flag with a white cross unfurled in the wind, and below it was a decoration of beautiful garlands made of flowers and green leaves.

A view of Cruz Bay, St. Jan, Danish West Indies © The Royal Library of Denmark

The town was adorned too with festoons and flags, not only with the Danish national colors but those of other nations as well. It was a colorful display of unity for this special occasion as everyone looked forward to the day's events.

Built at the edge of the pier was an arch with an oversized board suspended from its center. On the one side, the words, *Welcome H.R.H. Prince Carl* were written, and on the other, *God Bless Our Noble Prince!*

Greeting the Prince

The crowd's enthusiasm was palpable as they all gathered together at the landing-place, excited to meet this imperial Prince. This was the first royal visitor to the island, and many had no idea what to expect.

Prince Carl arriving in Cruz Bay, St. John in 1896 © The Royal Library of Denmark

The women dressed beautifully for the occasion, adorned in long white, cotton-lace skirts with decorative straw hats. Some of the men wore long-sleeved shirts under dark dress-coats despite the high temperature. Perhaps their Panama hats kept them cool in the hot sun.

As the royal party approached, they were quickly surrounded and those who met the Prince's gaze gracefully bowed and smiled at him.

The children, *'cleanly and tidily dressed',* were too excited to stand still. They feverishly waved their home-made banners and flags back and forth, to get his attention.

This was the first time they welcomed a visitor of this distinction and they were eager to get a closer glimpse of him.

One of the ladies gracefully stepped forward with pride and presented the Prince with a nosegay, a small bouquet of scented flowers she had picked herself.

In center: Prince Carl
© The Danish Royal Library

There was such an incredible outpouring of joy and warmth for their noble guest. When he accepted the flowers, he smiled broadly in joyful appreciation.

Touring the Ship

Prince Carl thanked everyone for their kind hospitality and in a gesture of gratitude, invited those in attendance to tour his ship. Over 130 people accepted his invitation and stood in line near the lifeboats for the rare opportunity.

As the small tenders crisscrossed the shallow waters to take everyone to the boarding ladders, Danish Officers waited on the top step to greet them. Immediately, the ship's orchestra began to play, welcoming everyone when they stepped forward onto the breezeway.

The Danish Cruiser, *Fyen*, anchored in Cruz Bay in 1896 © The Royal Library of Denmark

As the visitors dispersed for a closer look around, the children ran between the rigging to the bow, then to the aft deck, and peeked through all the hatches as they explored their new surroundings.

Despite being avid sailors themselves, they had never seen rigging ropes so thick or masts so high! Little smiling faces glanced around every corner in amazement, thrilled by their discoveries.

Residents celebrate Prince Carl's arrival on St. John © The Royal Library of Denmark

As the *'charming music'* permeated through the ship, the women embraced their partners and danced, swaying their long skirts back and forth in a festive gesture of fun and merriment. What a happy time they all had!

Residents celebrate Prince Carl's arrival on St. John © The Royal Library of Denmark

A Scenic Canter through the Countryside

While the ship's crew entertained the residents, the dignitaries embarked on a scenic canter through the countryside. It was a quick chance to marvel at some of St. John's panoramic beauty before they departed.

They stopped at *Estate Rustenberg* first, a former sugar estate, where the unfolding vista was unsurpassable.

The silent spectacle spoke volumes. At almost 800 feet above sea level, the view of dotted hills spotted with tall canes was breathtaking.

On their return ride, they paused at *Estate Susannaberg* briefly, where acres of cocoa trees were being cultivated. John E. Lindqvist had erected an arch with the words, *Welcome Our Prince,* as a surprise for him.

Unforgettable Memories

When the Prince returned to Cruz Bay, he was visibly moved by the great effort the community put forth in making him feel welcome.

Heartfelt moments of goodbye and farewell were exchanged. Despite the short time together, their bond of friendship was sincere and gratifying. That evening, as the ship sailed out of sight, they left many new friends with unforgettable memories of one of the happiest days in the island's history.

Students and their teacher await Prince Carl's arrival © The Royal Library of Denmark

It was truly an extraordinary day, both for the Prince and the people of St. John, a memory they would all relive for a lifetime.

Purchasing the Estates ~ 1897

The following year—in 1897—after Prince Carl's visit, Eugène rode up to the knoll on *Annaberg Estate* and paused by the lookout where the horizon stretched beyond to the British Virgins. The scene moved him beyond words.

A view of the British Virgins from Leinster Bay © The Royal Library of Denmark

Sitting in his saddle, not wanting to leave, he made an emotional decision that would change his life forever.

He decided to purchase the three estates, paying $3,100 in cash, and looked forward to the new livestock venture he would soon embark upon. For reasons unknown, the deed was recorded in his wife's name, Grizelda Flori Henri.

The properties encompassed 1,600 acres, all planted in luxuriant guinea grass. They were fenced all around and subdivided into ten enclosures.

The view from the shoreline was breathtaking! The channel between the islands lay before them, and hours could be spent watching the sloops traverse the narrow waterways.

There was an abundant supply of water for the livestock, and large troughs were filled by windmill pumps. *Leinster Bay* was perfect for raising cattle since it was known to have the *'most grass'*.

Three hundred head of cattle grazed along its rolling hills, along with horses, donkeys, and sheep. Besides the main dwelling house, the sloop, *Sea Bird* was also included in the sale.

Eugène was happy with the arrangements. He spent as much time as he could with his young family at the estates. Besides the two boys, Harry and Francois, he brought Excelman, Denis and Marie Herminie, all under the age of twelve.

As my mother and I listened to Aimee's story, we sat on the edge of our seats. We knew Eugène was our direct relation but had never heard this account before.

Aimee's final tantalizing tale that she shared with us would be one of intrigue and betrayal, a story that would lead to Eugène's untimely death.

Rumors of Deception ~ 1899

One rainy day in August, Aimee said, after the passing of the *San Ciriaco* hurricane, Eugène received unsettling news concerning his livestock investment. An acquaintance informed him that the caretaker overlooking his estates was clandestinely selling some of his cattle.

Why are you troubling my poor brain?, he probably asked the bearer of bad news, before he became visibly agitated and then angry when he heard further details of the report.

Pacing back and forth, gripping his ivory-topped walking stick that he used to gently clear his steps of sitting children, he devised a plan of what he would do when he confronted the caretaker.

Like his father, Eugène was a man with many flavorful words, both in English and French. He had a great command of his goose-feathered quill, and very likely wrote the caretaker a fiery letter, before he hired a sloop to take him and his two boys to *Leinster Bay* to confront him. His son, Harry, was twelve years old (Aimee's father) and his brother, Francois, younger.

As Eugène approached with his accusations, the caretaker *'denied the assertions in the most formal way'* and claimed to have no knowledge of the situation. He reassured his employer numerous times that the cattle counts were accurate, hoping it would quell his anger.

Eugène didn't believe all his flattery and promises. He was still enraged and *'with true Christian feelings, he pitied the unfortunate soul'* that would dare to take advantage of him! He believed the poor fellow had a motive for his *variance of the truth.*

As the caretaker tried again to appease Eugène, it became obvious his efforts were of no use. To Eugène, the caretaker's defense was *bosh tomfoolery!*

Eugène was reminded of a French saying he once heard, *"Truth lies, it is said, at the bottom of a well, and it is not everyone who can draw it up; sometimes, however, cela saute aux yeux."* That is to say, it is quite obvious.

According to Aimee, when the arguing subsided, Eugène was offered something to eat before he departed for the long sail back to St. Thomas. Nothing was offered to his two sons who remembered and spoke of this later amongst family members.

The Alleged Poisoning

It was alleged that as the meal was being prepared, a poisonous substance must have been surreptitiously mixed into the preparation. Relatives speculated that it was either powdered glass or fine horsehair, two popular age-old beliefs.

Although powdered glass was thought to cause irreparable harm long ago, over the years, it has since been disproven. Pieces of glass slivers could damage the internal organs, but the likelihood of someone continuing to consume a meal with non-soluble particles was unlikely.

One possible poison that may have been added to Eugène's food was arsenic, the chief poison of the Victorian era. The victim died in horrible agony, sometimes suffering a lingering death and sometimes more quickly according to the dose administered.

Certainly, arsenic was used with great success to rid the island of rats. Homeowners used to place the poison in sprat by removing one of its eyes and filling the socket with the deadly substance. This process preserved the fish long enough to kill lots of rodents.

The Apothecary was a familiar supplier to households in the late 1800s but was forbidden to sell poison to anyone without a prescription from a medical doctor. The police authorities, however, were known to use poisons to kill unwanted animals.

We may never know what happened to Eugène on that fateful day, but hours after his journey home, he became very ill. He languished for more than a week with stomach pains before succumbing to his ailment, eventually dying on August 26, 1899. He was sixty-four years of age.

Talk spread throughout the town when the boys shared their stories of what they believed happened. They remembered how uneasy they felt when nothing was offered to them for lunch. Suspicions continued to mount, but no accusations were ever printed publicly in the newspaper.

A family member in Tortola wrote Eugène a letter after hearing how suddenly sick he had become. *'How are you getting on?'* he asked on August 23, 1899.

After Eugène passed away, he sent a letter to Eugène's son-in-law inquiring, *'How is the Lagarde family getting on since his death?'*

This was a very difficult time for the family. As they grieved for Eugène, who was a husband, father, uncle and more, no one close to him knew exactly what happened to him.

Eugène's Obituary Notice

Eugène's obituary announcement was published in *The Bulletin* newspaper on August 28, 1899.

"Mr. L.E. de Lagarde, a well-known resident and proprietor, departed this life yesterday morning, after a short illness, in the 64th year of his age.

Deceased was for some time a member of the Colonial Council and for several years filled the post of Consul General of Haiti, with headquarters at Barbados, an office created by the late President Salomon. The funeral took place in the afternoon and was largely attended."

A Possible Culprit

Thanks again to David Knight Sr.'s research, Eugène's probate records and other documents related to the *Leinster Bay Estate* were discovered at *The National Archives* in Washington DC.

Those documents revealed that in June of 1882, when Antoine Anduze owned the estates, there was an overseer on the property with a dubious history.

In a sworn statement, Jacob S. Hill, the Quarter Officer, stated that *"Francois Calliste has repeatedly threatened violence and pointed firearms at people in the neighborhood."* He said, *"ever since he shot Peter Thomas at Leinster Bay, he was known by one and all to be a dangerous man."*

John Wells testified that whenever Calliste visited *Estate Brown* to redeem impounded cattle, *"he was never without arms on his person."*

Additional records revealed that as late as 1885, Calliste was still representing Mr. Anduze when the Annaberg boundary line was surveyed. With a gap of fourteen to seventeen years between those reports and Eugène's death in 1899, it's impossible to know if Francois Calliste was responsible. To this day, Eugène's death remains shrouded in mystery.

Grizelda Flore Henri

Only the year before Eugène died—on June 2, 1898—he and Grizelda were married. He was sixty-three years of age and she was fifty-four. They had been with each other for a long time and were raising five children together.

When Eugène's estates were probated, Grizelda attempted to secure them for herself as his widow. This did not prove advantageous for her as his third wife because Eugène died intestate. Danish laws advocated for the eldest son of the first marriage to inherit their father's property.

Interestingly, three days before Eugène's death, Grizelda filed a *Bill of Sale* for the three St. John estates, transferring them to her sister, Mrs. Mathurine Gerard for $2,200. The deed was dated the previous year, May 8, 1898. Her reasons for waiting fifteen months to make the filing at the *Office of the Recorder of Deeds* are a mystery.

On September 5, 1899, Mrs. Gerard made an offer to the Dealings Court of St. Thomas in which she would transfer back, without compensation, the three St. John properties to the estate of the deceased, which included Grizelda.

Family members still maintained, however, that Grizelda lost everything after Eugène died.

Grizelda Henri-de Lagarde, originally from the town of Marigot in St. Martin, French West Indies

Auctioning Eugène's Estates ~ 1899

Within two months of Eugène's death, all of his St. Thomas and St. John estates were auctioned and sold.

His firstborn son, Joseph Matthew Poniatowsky de Lagarde, would have received everything under Danish Law, but he died the previous year. His second son, John Romain de Lagarde, born in 1864, was believed to have inherited the estates. He was living in Paris when he heard the sad news and hired two Danish lawyers in St. Thomas to liquidate all of his father's properties.

It was reported that the unscrupulous lawyers he hired took advantage of the situation and did not reveal the total received for Eugène's properties. Since John Romain was overseas, he had no way of knowing their true value. Family members remarked that it would have been better for Grizelda not to have married Eugène, because she would have been able to keep the lands he gave her.

For many years prior, Grizelda was his mistress, and after Eugène's wife, (Georgina Sylvanie de Lagarde) died in 1868, she moved in and occupied the residence with him. Now, the contents of their personal home together were being claimed to pay Eugène's debts, with the proceeds going to his second son by his first marriage.

According to the Probate records that David Knight Sr. discovered, a detailed inventory of the contents of their home was performed. The more valuable items on the household list of over 100 entries were Eugène's pieces of jewelry. A large diamond ring was valued at $42.25 and an eighteen-karat, gold repeater watch was $35.

The more moderately priced pieces were the mahogany presses, tea tables, card tables, dining tables, bookcases, walnut chairs, seat rockers, as well as a large oil painting of the French President, Sadi Carnot.

President Sadi Carnot

President Carnot was a French statesman who served as the President of France from 1887 until his assassination in 1894.

He was someone Eugène admired very much.

The detailed inventory provided an insight into Eugène's life that we never would have known.

Interestingly, the gold medals, epaulets, and swords that his great-granddaughter, Esther, admired when she was a young girl, were never itemized in the household inventory.

President Sadi Carnot © Britannica.com

The Purchasers of Eugène's Estates ~ 1899

From David Knight Sr.'s research, we learned the names of the various individuals that acquired Eugène's St. John properties.

The three estates went to:

- Mr. Israel Levin, a merchant of St. Thomas. He purchased *Estate Abrams Fancy* for $800.
- Carl E. Francis purchased *Estate Annaberg* for $1,700, and
- Henry Clen purchased *Estate Leinster Bay* for $930.00, with sixty-three heads of cattle, plus auction costs.

Eugène owned three livestock estates for two years. He was the first direct ancestor to appreciate the beautiful, rich landscapes indigenous to St. John. Unfortunately, his love for the land and the livestock business contributed to the loss of his life.

Listening to Aimee share this story with us brought us closer. This was the first time we had met one another, and we bonded together over our love for our family's history.

Despite our ancestor's reputation as an unfaithful husband, he contributed to both branches of our families, giving each of us the precious gift of life.

THE *Second* GENERATION

Henry Osmond Creque

A Shareholder in the St. Thomas ~ St. John Plantation Co.

Chapter 3
Cultivating Cinnamon Bay
1903

During the nineteenth century, it was a customary practice in the islands for enterprising young men to learn a trade from a skilled master.

In 1876, Henry O. Creque, a teenager from Anegada, emigrated to St. Thomas to apprentice under Israel Levin, a Lithuanian merchant who ran a dry goods business on Main Street.

The knowledge Henry gained from working as a clerk under his tutelage proved to be invaluable. Everything he learned about operating a successful business was credited to Mr. Levin.

Ambitious as Henry was, he had already accumulated a small fortune with the sale of copper fittings from sunken ships. As a youth, he dove the wrecks surrounding his island home, taking what he found to sell in St. Thomas.

One of the ships he salvaged was quite noteworthy. It was the Royal British Mail steamer, *Paramatta*. Tragically, in 1859, the vessel hit the Horseshoe Reef on her maiden voyage and was a complete loss.

Rescue attempts of the *Paramatta* off Anegada, British Virgins © Illustrated London News

During the early 1880s, Henry met and fell in love with one of Eugène's first-born daughters, a young, beautiful girl with long, dark hair. Her name was Maria Dolores de Lagarde.

Maria Dolores de Lagarde, 1853 – 1914 © Valerie Sims

In 1884, Henry wrote a florid letter to Mr. de Lagarde, describing his *'deep and fervent affection for Miss Dolores.'* He asked for her *'hand in wedlock'* and promised him he would do everything to promote his daughter's welfare and happiness.

Eugène gave his blessing and the wedding took place on May 5, 1884, at the Danish Lutheran Church in St. Thomas. Witnessing the event were the two men he respected very much, Israel Levin and his father, John Bedford Creque of Anegada.

Shortly after their marriage, Maria gave birth to their only son together, Herman Ogilvie Creque, the author's great-grandfather.

Commodore Edmund S. Poe © The Navy and Army Illustrated, 1898

The Central Ironmongery ~ 1884

Later that year, Henry opened a new establishment selling everything from bags of flour and cornmeal to Imperial Beer and galvanized roofing tiles. He also provisioned visiting ships with food supplies and other necessities, anchoring alongside in secluded harbors to transfer the goods.

Provisioning Her Royal Majesty's Ships ~ 1900

One such rendezvous took place in the calm waters of the Virgin Gorda Sound in the British Virgin Islands.

In December of 1900, Henry met with Commodore, Edmund S. Poe of the *West Indies Training Squadron*, belonging to Her Majesty. On this occasion, he tendered his ship, the *HMS Crescent*, with fresh beef, including steers, oxen, veal, and mutton from his commercial farm at Norman Island. He also supplied pumpkins, Halifax potatoes, and Madeira onions.

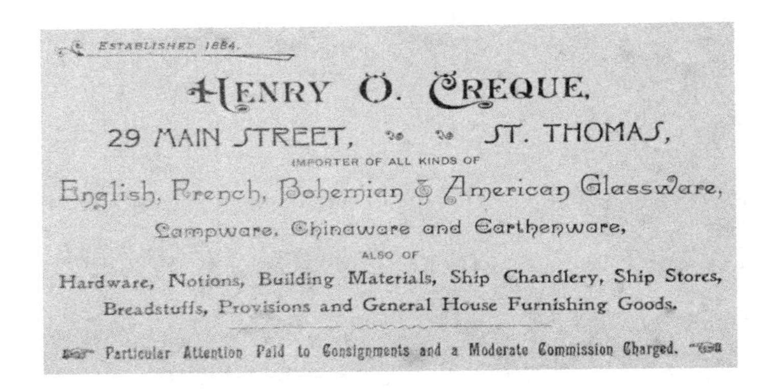

ESTABLISHED 1884.

HENRY O. CREQUE,

29 MAIN STREET, ST. THOMAS,

IMPORTER OF ALL KINDS OF

English, French, Bohemian & American Glassware,

Lampware, Chinaware and Earthenware,

ALSO OF

Hardware, Notions, Building Materials, Ship Chandlery, Ship Stores,

Breadstuffs, Provisions and General House Furnishing Goods.

Particular Attention Paid to Consignments and a Moderate Commission Charged.

Henry's position as a General Commission Merchant proved successful; Commander Poe was greatly satisfied with his service and *'genially attested to this with his personal signature.'*

According to the *St. Croix Avis* newspaper, Henry was among *'the best-known men of the community.' 'He was an enterprising man, one that may be termed self-made, having begun his commercial life on a most modest scale, developing it to its present dimensions.'*

The St. Thomas & St. John Plantation Co. ~ 1903

As Henry's businesses flourished, he purchased hundreds of acres of land in the Danish West Indies and the British Virgin Islands; however, he did not purchase any St. John estates personally, nor did his wife inherit any of her father's properties.

Instead, he became an active member and shareholder in *The St. Thomas and St. John Plantation Company*. This company was responsible for purchasing several estates on St. John, one of which was *Cinnamon Bay Estate*. In 1902, when meetings were held concerning this new enterprise, contributions and subscriptions from community members poured in.

Prominent citizens like Secretary Lars Christian Helweg-Larsen, who later became the island's Governor, J.P. Thorsen, A.H. Riise, Louis Delinois, Israel Levin, Carl V. LaBeet and John Muller purchased 'A' shares at $100 each. Others purchased B and C shares at $50 and $25 respectively.

Henry Osmond Creque became an "A shareholder" on June 22, 1903.

The Company's Objective

The company's objective was to promote agricultural pursuits in the islands by cultivating several fruits, including bananas, mangos, coconuts, pineapples, and oranges. They also planted cocoa plants, onions, pigeon peas, tanias, cassava, and limes.

This endeavor was helpful to the local community because it provided employment to a number of laborers and created a demand for carpenters, masons, and other skilled workers.

Onions, Cotton and Bay Rum ~ 1904

John E. Lindqvist, a planter cultivating *America Hill*, went to St. Kitts to purchase a quantity of cotton seed for the estates. Seven acres of pineapples and twenty-one acres in bananas were already planted, and the company planned to add more, including seven acres of cotton.

Because there were not enough workers available, an additional twenty-four contract laborers were brought from St. Kitts to work on the company's farms. With their help, *Cinnamon Bay* produced 8,000 to 10,000 pounds of onions under this initiative.

One particular onion grown on the estate was shown to a newspaper editor and he couldn't believe the size of it. It weighed a pound a half! This unusually large onion, he said, was *'a fine, sound quality.'*

A Tour of the Crops Under Cultivation

Word spread to St. Thomas about their success and curious planters visited the estate to gather ideas for their farms. A brief account of their visit was found in *The Bulletin* newspaper:

The banana fields © The Royal Library of Denmark, Album of Gov. Helweg-Larsen

'After landing at Cruz Bay, we found horses in readiness and rode to Enighed first, where we saw large tracts of Sea Island cotton in full bloom as well as some of the cotton that had been reaped.

'We visited Hawksnest where an old-fashioned cane-grinding apparatus operated by mule power was being used. We then proceeded to Cinnamon Bay where the onions were flourishing.

'Our next stop was Maho Bay with its fine crop of canes and bananas and a short ride further to Mary's Point, where we saw large tracts of land under fine cultivation.

'It was a day well spent and we hoped our brother-planters would have the same privilege to see what we are doing in St. Thomas.

'We gathered a lot of good ideas from our visit and saw lots of cultivations including potatoes, onions, yams, cassava, pineapples, bananas, canes, cotton, and many other things.'

After admiring the beautifully cultivated plots, they agreed, *'the onion cultivation was a grand success.'*

Growing Onions

Although they were thriving, onions were not easy to cultivate. The soil had to be well-drained and prepared first with manure, then forked at least twelve inches deep to pulverize everything so that all the lumps were broken up for the onions to grow.

Daily raking was needed too to keep the weeds from taking over, or they would deprive the onion bulbs of air and light, affecting their proper development.

Despite the laborious preparation, the agricultural department urged the estate proprietors and small landholders to take up the growing of onions on a larger, more systematic scale.

They felt the Virgin Islands' soil, with its texture and moisture content, was perfect for this endeavor. So perfect, they practically gave the onion bulbs away at three cents for 100 plants.

The Bay Rum Business

Four years later, the Plantation Company went into the bay rum business and made a *'fine article'* there as well. Unfortunately, many of the St. Thomas estates suffered losses due to the extensively dry weather.

In a desperate effort, the company moved some of their St. Thomas stock to St. John, where the weather conditions were more favorable.

They watched the barometer faithfully, hoping it would fall and be an indication of impending rain.

"With the weather, as with human affairs, there was no telling what a day might bring forth."

A sloop at anchor © Creque Family Archives

The Sinking of the Sloop, Pearl ~ 1899

In addition to Henry's involvement with the company, he was also the registered agent for many of the inter-island boats traveling back and forth to St. John.

During the early hours, before the passing of the San Ciriaco hurricane, Captain William Thomas lost his sailboat, the *Pearl.* He was an experienced sailor, known throughout the islands as Captain Willie of Cruz Bay.

While attempting to find shelter for his boat, he sailed from Caneel Bay to another part of St. John, very likely Hurricane Hole, but didn't make it. The vessel capsized from the strong gusty winds, and two passengers lost their lives.

Over the two days that the hurricane crossed over the Caribbean islands, including Puerto Rico, it killed nearly 3,300 people!

Henry came quickly to Captain Willie's aid. He posted a subscriber list in his St. Thomas store, *The Central Ironmongery*, for those who wished to donate to help the distraught captain.

By August 12, $112 was raised. It was sufficient to cover three-quarters of the purchase sum required for a replacement boat. Henry publicly thanked all who were so generous.

"The ready response to the appeal maintains the well-known reputable liberality of St. Thomas in cases of this kind."

Captain Willie was soon sailing again with a brand-new vessel which he used as a mail boat between the islands. He named the new craft, *Juliet* and was grateful to Mr. Creque for his kindness.

The Cruz Bay Dock © Creque Family Archives

The Sinking of the Sloop, Success ~ 1912

Although happy to have assisted the captain, Henry had problems of his own. Some of his engagements did not go as planned and resulted in losses for his company.

One of these was an interesting rendezvous that took place off the western end of St. John in late November 1912.

Henry sold ninety cases of tobacco on consignment to a gentleman in Guadeloupe and sent a couple of sailing boats with the cargo to meet with a larger sloop near Cruz Bay that would deliver the goods to the French colony.

They transferred the merchandise and sailed away, reaching as far as Virgin Gorda, where the boat stranded and wrecked. Interestingly, the doomed vessel was called, *Success.*

An Eyewitness's Account

James Lawrence, an eyewitness, told the following tale:
"We took in tobacco in Danish waters near St. Jan, the Westward end, and we were nearer St. Jan than St. Thomas harbor.

"The tobacco was brought by an English sailing boat coming from St. Thomas. I say English because after they left, they sailed straight up for Tortola. They had gone to St. Thomas to sell fish and brought the tobacco on their way back."

Of the ninety cases sent, only thirty-seven were salvageable. Unfortunately, when those were left to sit in storage without ventilation, they too perished. When Henry was finally contacted to determine the tobacco's quality, he said, *'it was no good.'*

Undaunted, he continued to ship goods he sold through a labyrinth of inter-island, coastal waterways, and remained very involved in matters that concerned St. John's prosperity and betterment.

THE *Third* GENERATION

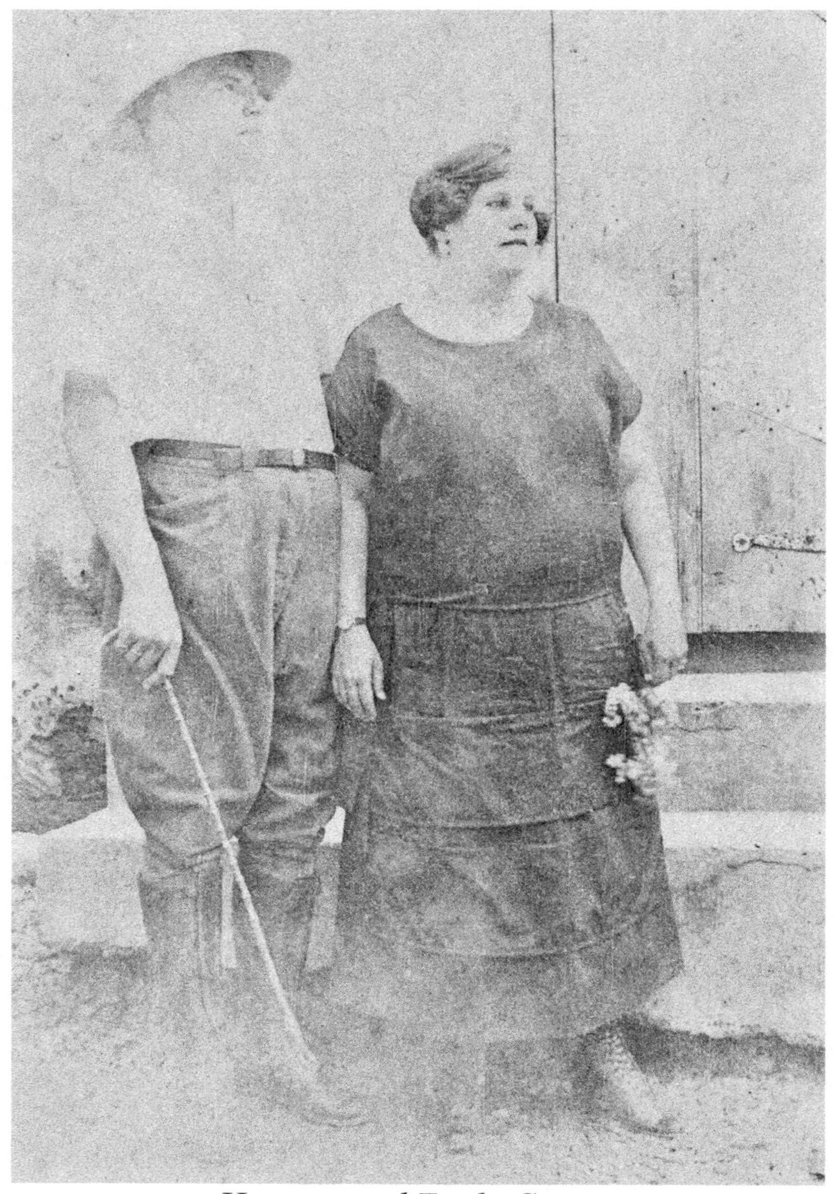

Herman and Emily Creque

Owners of Great & Little Lamesure • Concordia • Bakkero Parforce • Hope • Misgunst • Bordeaux • Cabritte Horn

Chapter 4

Living at Lamesure Estate 1922

Henry and his wife Maria had one child together that survived to adulthood, and in 1920, their son fell in love with St. John too, becoming the third generation with ties to the island.

Off to England for an Education

Herman was educated in St. Thomas then attended Bowden College in Cheshire, England, when he was sixteen. Max E. Trepuk, a family friend, accompanied the young boy on his travels to Europe.

'Herman was an excellent worker with great promise', wrote one of his teachers on his July 1900 report card. Indeed, he was right. When he returned to St. Thomas, he joined his father and became very focused on the details of running his companies.

Herman was a quiet and reserved young man who sat quietly with his Dad when he accompanied him to his business meetings. In addition to *The Central Ironmongery*, his father owned the *Creque Department Store* in 1905 and later, the *Creque Marine Railway* on Hassel Island in 1910. Herman sat in on many of the meetings his father had with the Board of Directors after his bid for the railway was successful.

The two were very close, not only affectionate as father and son, but also as friends and business partners. The skills Herman learned from his father helped him considerably when accounting for both his receivables and expenses. He knew immediately when payments were delinquent, or merchandise had not been received after its purchase.

When his father sailed to New York on the s/s Guiana, they shared many long letters back and forth concerning the arrival of various lumber shipments and other goods for their establishments.

Herman liked to keep abreast of worldwide news, as well as local happenings. He was *'The Boss'* to his employees, firm and assertive, yet his softer side wrote poems for his children and teased and joked around with them. With his grandchildren, he was playful, often sharing stories about the island's history with them.

According to his granddaughter, Diane, every afternoon, he would sit on the wharf and say his rosary. He was very spiritual and converted to Catholicism from Protestantism at the urging of his wife.

He cared about his community and joined many civic organizations and fundraising committees.

One particular passion he learned from his father was to invest in properties as long-term investments. The funds he earned from his businesses were all funneled toward this endeavor.

Herman had a particular preference for coastline properties, which over time, increased in value. Many of the lands he acquired both in the British Virgin Islands and Danish West Indies were purchased at reduced prices through auction houses.

Estate Lime Tree Bay ~ 1920

Herman's first purchase of St. John property was eight acres of *Estate Lime Tree Bay* on the eastern end of the island, also known as Haulover Bay. It was owned by Oswald Waldemar George and his wife, who was a teacher at the Emmaus Country School.

Herman paid $500 for the land. The two men met when Oswald invested in a sunken sailboat that went to the bottom during the hurricane of 1916. He brought it to the marine railway for repairs. As a fine carpenter, Oswald spent quite a bit of time every day restoring the old boat to its former glory.

Oswald George
© National Archives, Washington, DC

It wasn't long before another beautiful property became available.

Herman's second purchase on St. John was *Estate Lamesure,* tucked behind a faraway cove on the southeastern end of the island. It was so secluded and remote that the easiest way of accessing it was by boat, otherwise, it was a long, bumpy ride by horseback from Cruz Bay.

Herman, like his maternal grandfather, Eugène, admired the natural, unspoiled beauty the island offered.

Lamesure was a working estate with groves of various cultivations. Below are a few of its proprietors and the improvements and development plans of those who owned the property before and after Herman's purchase.

Landowners of Lamesure Estate

- William H. Marsh, 1877 – 1906
- Count Henrik Grevenkop-Castenskiold, 1906 – 1920
- Charles Seymour Westbrook, 1920 – 1921
- Lieutenant Seth F.H. Lagerstadt, 1921 – 1922
- Herman O. Creque and his family, 1922 – 1953
- Frank & David Stick and their investors, 1953 – 1954
- Jackson Hole Preserve, Inc., 1954 – 1956
- The Virgin Islands National Park, 1956 – Today

William H. Marsh, Esq. ~ 1877

According to research by Charles Hatch, Jr., William H. Marsh was an Englishman from Tortola who later became a prominent St. John Councilman. He managed the *Estates of Parforce* and *Reef Bay* for several years, and around 1861, converted the cane-grinding operation from horsepower to steam power. When *Reef Bay Estate* came up for auction in 1864, he purchased the property for himself, becoming its new owner. In 1877, he acquired *Lamesure Estate.*

According to his report, the *Reef Bay Sugar Factory* was in operation for many years until, in 1908, the intensive sugar cultivations ceased in favor of cattle raising.

Estate Reef Bay Sugar Factory © The Library of Congress

The change may have been the result of a serious accident that took place at the factory and claimed the life of one of the young workers. *Lightbourn's Mail Notes* carried the horrific news of what happened on March 7, 1908.

"A sad accident occurred at the *Estate Riff Bay* on Saturday afternoon. While a young lad, aged 15 years, was picking up canes near the revolving fly wheel of the engine, he somehow got caught in the cogs of the wheel, and in less than a minute, before any help could be rendered, was crushed to death, his body being completely cut in two."

Count Henrik Castenskiold, 1862 - 1921 © The Royal Library of Denmark

Count Henrik Grevenkop-Castenskiold

William Marsh first met Count Henrik Grevenkop-Castenskiold when he arrived on the island after a business trip to Mexico in February of 1904.

Count Henrik was an interesting person, being a member of the Danish Legation in London and a distant relative of the Royal Family of Denmark.

Count Henrik Purchases the Estates ~ 1904

The two men shared many lengthy discussions about the economic conditions of the island and as a result of their talks, Count Henrik decided to invest in St. John.

He had been thinking about it for quite some time, ever since the Danish Royal Commissioners visited the island the year before to learn more about the needs of the community.

He purchased Mr. Marsh's estates, which included *Lamesure, Bordeaux, Hope, Parforce, Cabritte Horn, Bakkero,* and *Misgunst* for a total sum of $6,000, in November 1904.

Count Henrik envisioned this transaction as an opportunity to help those less fortunate, endeavoring to create an industry to benefit the local inhabitants. He planned to accomplish this by planting lemons and limes, which were hearty and could withstand the humid weather.

Count Henrik was very familiar with the Danish West Indies, having had a third great-grandfather who once lived at *Estate Pearl* on the western end of St. Thomas.

During the eighteenth century, his ancestor was known to be a friend of the Moravians when they first arrived to minister amongst the slaves. As a matter of interest, it was at *Estate Pearl,* where the first slaves were baptized.

A New House ~ 1905

During the summer months, Count Henrik was eager to get started on this new venture. A portion of the *Lamesure* land was cleared in preparation for the arrival of a new, wooden-framed structure that was built on St. Thomas and transported in sections by boat. Once these improvements and others were underway, he planned a month-long visit.

In 1907, a popular and very well-respected gentleman from the community assumed the management of his estates in his absence.

Alice and Alfred White at Lamesure Estate © The Royal Library of Denmark

Alfred and Alice White

Alfred White was a Colonial Council member, active on both the Municipal Committee and the School Board, and with the support and admiration of many. He was someone Count Henrik trusted completely.

On New Year's Eve in 1905, Alfred wed Miss Alice Penn, and together they occupied the main dwelling. Arthur Davis, a trusted laborer, was hired to assist with caring for the animals.

Alfred was excited about this opportunity because he felt Count Henrik shared his same ideals. Together, they would be able to accomplish more than most.

Count Henrik's Visit ~ 1907

After a long and uneventful passage, the Count arrived aboard the *s/s St. Thomas*, which anchored off St. Croix.

From there, he booked his passage to St. Thomas on the motor schooner, *Viking*, then hired a small sloop to take him directly to *Lamesure Bay*.

The *Viking* had been sent from Denmark to replace the old, faithful schooner, *Vigilant,* which needed repairs. It took the *Viking* thirty-seven days crossing from Dover, where she stopped on her way from Copenhagen.

The Danish schooner, *Viking*

The new, steel-built vessel was ninety-one feet in length and offered a spacious and comfortable saloon. She was under the command of Captain Stromberg before Captain Hassell took the helm.

Count Henrik preferred this new yacht and the cool November month when the Tradewinds were blowing.

It was a long, arduous journey for him, but his scenic and secluded estate had all the amenities he desired, a panoramic view, lush, fertile grounds, and a working enterprise that he hoped would help the local community.

Cultivating Limes and Lemons

Early cultivations on *Lamesure Estate* included acres of sugarcane and cotton, grown on the northwest part of the property.

Count Henrik planned to cultivate lemons and limes instead, which he knew grew easily and could withstand the dry conditions. They were perfect for this endeavor and proven successful in nearby Tortola. Almost 800 barrels were gathered there by small proprietors and sold to the Experiment Station for export.

For three years, the laborers worked hard tilling the soil, and under ideal growing conditions, the lime trees produced a nice crop.

Count Henrik was pleased to see all the improvements undertaken during his absence. Plenty of sunlight, adequate moisture, and well-draining soil was important in caring for the orchards, or the leaves would die, and the fruit would spoil.

In June and July, the sweetly-scented white flowers blossomed, indicating a ripening fruit. When they faded and fell to the ground, a nut-like pod the size of a pea, hung in small clusters below.

Within a short time, the estate had 2,000 lime trees near fruiting. With their glossy, green leaves and fragrant flowers, the hillsides were beautiful with rows of ripening groves.

The idea was to crush the fruit, extract the juice into concentrated form, and export it to Europe. The refuse was also of value and would be used to feed the cattle and manure the land.

The Medicinal Properties of Limes

Long ago, lime trees were planted by royal decree, since they were valued for their medicinal properties. Epilepsy and other nervous illnesses were said to be cured by simply sitting under the tree.

A soothing tea made from the dried leaves was considered an *'effective treatment for headaches, insomnia, and a nervous disposition.'*

Sea Island Cotton

Before Count Henrik purchased the estates, Alfred made attempts to grow Sea Island cotton from seeds received from the Danish Plantation Company. Three acres were dedicated to this endeavor, which turned out to be *'a very fine article.'*

He intended to extend and develop the cultivation of cotton as well. *'Count Henrik was principally interested in any well-suited industry, that would benefit the island's inhabitants.'*

When bales of the cotton arrived in England, they were favorably classified as *fine* and realized a price of fourteen pence per pound. It was evident that Count Henrik had a *'deep, vested interest in the island by his endeavors to do something on a scale that would be of general benefit.'*

The Aarhus Exhibition in Denmark ~ 1909

As the cultivations were underway, an interesting exhibition was being planned in Aarhus, Denmark. It was called, *The Danish National Exhibition of 1909*. There, industry crafts and cultural products from around the world would be exhibited for thousands to see.

Count Henrik penned a letter to Alfred about gathering various handicrafts and produce from his estates to participate in the exhibition. Proud of all the accomplishments thus far, he was very excited about this opportunity.

Making baskets on St. John © A Lightbourn Postcard

Before the articles were sent to Denmark, one of the local newspaper editors had the chance to see them first. He was *'agreeably surprised'* by their quality. The articles were not very numerous but were such that would attract both *'attention and interest.'* There was a fine grade of cocoa from Louis Delinois' *Estate Susannaberg*, and pretty lace and thread work by Miss Izza Penn and Miss Lottie Clen from *Estate Leinster Bay.*

Miss Clen later attended a school in Copenhagen for Needlework and was one of seven students to receive prizes of fifty kroner each for fancy-lacework. In 1912, she was the *"first West Indian to receive such a prize."*

The list from *Bordeaux* included curios in the way of star-shaped fish-pots, straw fans, hats, sticks, calabashes, and different sorts of preserved fruits. Also included were samples of coffee, bay oil, Guavaberry liqueur, and distilled Guavaberry rum, the latter made from the blackberries, but bottled clear.

Specimens of red and yellow ochre, found on the island and used for coating walls, were also among the estate's exhibits.

The editor made a special note of Alice White's contribution, praising her collection of Spanish-work. The so called "Spanish-work" was a kind of embroidery done by "pulling threads in fine canvas and silk." Mrs. White also made *'two exquisite silk waists'* and a *'beautiful lace hat.'*

Setting fish traps off St. John © A Postcard

These specimens of work, he believed, would be *'difficult to excel'*. St. John, then, would be represented by a small but select display. With *'much energy and enthusiasm'*, Holger Jacobsen and Luther Stakemann collected and forwarded all the articles to Denmark.

The Prizes Awarded

As anticipated, the Aarhus Exhibition was considered a success!

- A.H. Riise of St. Thomas won the silver medal for his fine bay rum elixir.
- As anticipated, Mrs. White was awarded a diploma and a bronze medal for her submissions.

Everyone was excited when one of the Crown Princesses shook the winner's hands. It was a glorious evening with 500 guests attending the dinner ceremony. Displayed were approximately 1,850 individual works by various artists and craftsmen from around the world. Incredibly, the exhibition attracted 650,000 visitors!

The St. John community was happy to know that in one of the two largest halls in Denmark was their modest, but prized exhibition of homespun handicrafts.

A Visit to Estate Lamesure ~ 1910

The following year, Count Henrik returned for a seventeen-day holiday. This time, he brought his new wife along on the East Asiatic Company's steamer, the *s/s St. Thomas* from Copenhagen.

Her name was Anne Margrethe (Daisy) Grevenkop-Castenskiold. Their timing was perfect to see the orchards exploding with thousands of fruit-bearing trees. Count Henrik was very happy and felt a sense of personal fulfillment, knowing he was helping others. Everything was going as planned. After a productive and somewhat restful holiday, the newlyweds departed for Trinidad on the *s/s Patagonia.*

Harvesting the Limes

By 1911, the limes were ready for harvesting. Alfred checked their ripeness by looking at their color, texture, and juiciness. When they changed from dark green to light green or yellow, he inspected their surface for smoothness. A wrinkled, rough skin indicated dry, overripe fruit, which was unusable.

Picking the limes was not as easy as one would think. Long thorns stood guard, and careless workers—who forgot to wear their thick gloves—received painful jabs. The juice was also very acidic, and constant exposure to the skin caused agonizing burns. Despite these setbacks, the workers persevered, knowing they would benefit in the end.

Limes © The Royal Library of Denmark

Purchasing More Limes

To keep the business sustainable, Alfred needed more limes than *Lamesure* produced. He placed advertisements in the newspaper and was able to purchase some from *Estate Lovenlund* near Magens Bay, as well as others from several estates in St. Croix.

He then distributed 5,000 young lime trees throughout the island, at no cost to the growers. John Lindqvist received 1,000, and William Marsh of *Estate Carolina,* 200.

Processing the Limes ~ 1911

Before processing, any damaged or unsuitable fruit was separated and discarded, the remainder being washed and cut in half. The apparatus, part of which was made in St. Thomas, was set up for starting the lime juice extraction. It consisted of a V-shaped hopper, which slowly dropped the pre-cut limes between two, moving, wooden rollers below. This process squeezed the fruit until the seeds fell onto a sieve while the juice dripped past them into a holding tank.

The lime juice may have been pasteurized since this process stopped the juice from turning brown during shipment. To accomplish this, the juice would have been boiled for one minute at ninety degrees Celsius in steel or earthenware pots.

Both Count Henrik and Alfred thought St. John an ideal place for growing limes and had high hopes for the success of the industry.

The First Shipment of Limes ~ 1912

A year later, the first shipment of concentrated lime juice was ready to be sent to London. It was exciting for them both to see their dreams come to fruition.

In 1913, Alfred and Alice welcomed a new baby boy into their family, which made them very happy. They both enjoyed working with Count Henrik and agreed that the production of limes could turn *'poverty into prosperity.'*

After all, it was successful on the Caribbean islands of Dominica and St. Lucia, and they wanted the people of St. John to succeed as well.

A 1911, preliminary count of the St. John census showed a total of 933 inhabitants, thirty-three residing in the town of Cruz Bay, and 900 in the country.

The newspapers continued to report on *Lamesure's* progress.

"We are glad to hear this, and we hope that the returns will be such as to succeed a furtherance of the industry to the island.

"Such an enterprise is praiseworthy, and we hope it may be pushed with such energy, and with the necessary cooperation of those who will ultimately share in the gain, that success may be a certain result."

A Visit by Countess Carstenskiold

In 1913, Countess Carstenskiold returned to the island aboard the steamer, *s/s Venetia* as a guest of the Governor and his family. She spent some quiet time at *Lamesure* with Alice and her family, but Count Henrik never returned. His visit in 1910 was the last time he saw his estates in such a verdant and healthy state.

Alfred and Alice White at the rear of the Lamesure home © The Royal Library of Denmark

The Hurricane of 1916

On October 9, 1916, the island had the misfortune of experiencing the most deplorable hurricane to ravage the island!

The morning opened with a light drizzle, and by noon, both rain and wind increased in intensity, until evening, when it began to blow with hurricane force. It carried death and destruction in its tract and brought misery, suffering, and ruin to many, especially the East-End community.

The author, Luther K. Zabriskie of the *Virgin Islands of the United States of America,* shared a vivid account of the hurricane conditions.

The state of things, he said, was *'appalling! There were no homes, no food, no fruit trees and no provision grounds left!*

View of Yawzi Point from the Lamesure Estate house © Creque Family Archives

Almost everything was flat! Boats, fishnets and all the fish-pots were gone. Desolation reigned!'

On *Bordeaux Hill*, only one or two houses were still standing.

Coral Bay was practically no more in existence since the church, parsonage and schoolhouse were gone. It was *'a marvel and a mercy'* that so few lives were lost.

Houses were lifted with people in them and thrown down, even rolled over, and yet only minor injuries were the result.

The Danish cruiser, *HMS Valkyrien,* was the first ship to arrive to render assistance. Seeing them on the horizon was a blessing!

The ship's doctor rode up to *Bordeaux* and gave medical attention to about fifteen persons, while his assistant went to East End and attended to several injured people there. The island suffered terribly, especially the buildings and crops, particularly the coconut, lime and bay trees.

'Of all the beautiful coconut palms, there was scarcely a dozen trees left on the whole island, even the beautiful coconut grove of Estate Trunk Bay was destroyed.'

The Sad Story of St. John

The island presented such a *'dreary and ruined appearance'*, very reminiscent of the damage inflicted by Hurricanes Irma and Maria in 2017.

It pierced the heart to see some of the people wandering, lost in a world of disbelief. The vegetation was scorched as if a hot blast had passed over it. Trees of every kind and size were uprooted in vast numbers, and those left standing were devoid of branches.

The broken trunks stood in bold relief against the landscape, with the ruins of buildings interspersed. The comparison was still more striking when one met the homeless, seeking in the ruins, one vestige of apparel or household utensil which might have escaped the wreck.

At *Lamesure Estate*, considerable damage was done to the main building, but the lime juice factory escaped untouched.

At *Bordeaux*, all the houses in the village were destroyed, except one. Several persons sustained injuries.

At *Leinster Bay*, the large dwelling that once belonged to Eugène had been completely wrecked *'with the loss of everything.'* Alfred's sailboat, *White Wings,* was thrown high and dry in the creek, but otherwise, it did not sustain much damage.

Fishermen, a postcard © The Royal Library of Denmark

For many days, the roads were impassable, even for pedestrians. Special credit was given to Alfred for the promptness with which he cleared them.

Several row boats were lost due to the unprecedented rise of the sea. Many of those that had been pulled ashore to a safe place were swept away by the waves.

It was a tragedy that left many in a destitute state of unparalleled suffering.

In a letter published by J.C. Lindqvist, the Quarter Officer, he had two words for St. John.

'Misery!! and Starvation!!'

He implored the good people of St. Thomas and St. Croix to donate whatever they could give, clothes, money, food, etc.

'In as much as ye have done it unto one of the least of My disciples, ye have done it unto Me.'

HMS Valkyrien © The Royal Library of Denmark

Danish Ship Brings Life-Saving Supplies ~1916

With the aid of Commander, Henri Konow of *HMS Valkyrien* and the Relief Committee, many were able to repair their homes and small cultivations. Besides life-saving medicines for the wounded, they brought galvanized sheets from Puerto Rico to replace the missing roofs. This was a huge help to the homeless and destitute.

The *Valkyrien* was a Danish ship stationed in the islands from 1915 when unrest and strikes were anticipated among the workers, and uncertainty about the eventual sale of the islands to the US left everyone feeling uneasy.

Before the ship dropped anchor in Coral Bay to land boxes of food and supplies, people were coming alongside in rowboats to beg for something to eat. The distraught victims were starving!

In 1917, a public meeting was held at the Grand Hotel in St. Thomas. There, it was unanimously agreed to send a note of thanks to the Minister of Finance for the *Valkyrien's* help. The people were *'exceedingly grateful to the gallant Commander for his zeal and attention'* paid to them in the days following the hurricane.

HMS Valkyrien's Crew © The Royal Library of Denmark

Helping the Volcano Victims in Martinique 1902

Not only did the *Valkyrien* and her crew help the hurricane survivors, but they also went to help the victims of Mount Pelé when it erupted in Martinique. It was a horrible disaster, unlike anything before, and it killed approximately 30,000 people.

The *Valkyrien* was one of the first ships dispatched from St. Thomas with *'cash, food, and medicines'* for the island. Incredibly, 46,000 pounds of foodstuffs and a large supply of medicines and surgical dressings were loaded onto the ship.

It was a '*mission of mercy'* for the gallant crew, and at the same time, one of *'great peril'* to help their unfortunate countrymen.

His Excellency, President Emile Loubet of France, showered his heartfelt appreciation on both the Governor of the islands and the Commander of the *Valkyrien*.

He bestowed the *Legion of Honor* upon both Governor Carl Emil Hedemann and Captain Hans Peter Holm. This was the highest order of distinction bestowed for merit.

Americans Show Interest in Lamesure ~ 1919

With a view of occupying a strategic position in the Caribbean, the US negotiated with Denmark for the transfer of the Danish West Indies. On March 31, 1917, they were ceded to the United States for $25,000,000.

At this time, several American businessmen took an interest in *Lamesure Estate* and sent Count Henrik unsolicited offers. Interested, he advised his business manager, Mr. Mietzefield, regarding a potential sale he believed might take place. Although he had no immediate plans to sell, he entertained the offers sent to him, one of which came from Charles Seymour Westbrook.

Charles had experience running his father's company, the *Rossie Iron Ore Mine* in New York. He also had mining interests in Mexico, where the two may have met.

Count Henrik's Asking Price

"Provided Mr. Westbrook was ready to pay $25,000.00, I would be willing to sell him the estates. I have on November 1st, through the Ministry of Foreign Affairs at Copenhagen, wired to the Danish Consul at St. Thomas, that a condition for the sale of the estates in St. Jan, is the cash payment of twenty-five thousand American Dollars. I will not take less, as I have no particular wish to sell the estate."

On February 14, 1920, he cabled Mr. Westbrook by Western Union from London.

'To Westbrook, Calumet Club, New York. Must ask for payment, entire sum. St. Thomas or New York, March 1st. Will otherwise not sell. Castenskiold, 5:12 pm.'

Long ago, when a property changed hands, previous deeds and supporting documents were given to the new owners. This letter from Count Henrik and documents from previous owners of *Estate Lamesure* and other estates were found among Herman's papers.

Charles S. Westbrook ~ 1920

Charles Westbrook agreed to Count Henrik's terms and paid the full asking price to his representative, Mr. G. Bech, the Consul General for Denmark in New York.

The Westbrooks purchased all of his holdings. Included, was a dwelling house with a stable and outhouse, laborer's cottages, tools, and all the livestock. Sadly, Count Henrik died just eighteen months after selling his estates, on August 28, 1921.

The Appraisement ~ 1921

For reasons unknown, the Westbrooks decided to sell the estates a year after purchasing them. When they requested an appraisement on the property from the Municipality, R.L. Pettigrew and Luther Stakemann, who owned *Mary's Point*, viewed the estate and valued it at $24,950.

A short time later, the Westbrooks found new purchasers, Lieutenant Seth F. H. Lagerstadt and his wife, Minnie.

Lieutenant Lagerstadt was an Ensign during the summer of 1920 when he and his wife visited St. Thomas aboard the *USS Kittery*.

(Note: In 1928, Charles Westbrook was injured when a taxi in which he was a passenger was involved in an accident with a truck. He suffered a fractured skull and died ten days later. He was survived by five children.)

Lieutenant Seth F.H. Lagerstadt ~ 1921

Lieutenant Lagerstadt also paid $25,000 for the estates. He was originally from Brockton, Massachusetts and a member of the US Naval Reserve Force.

At Rhode Island State College where he enrolled, his nickname on the football team was *Rabbit, the hot weather pitcher.* Perhaps the island's balmy weather and cool breezes enticed the twenty-nine-year-old to invest.

The Still © The Royal Library of Denmark, Tyge Hvass Collection

Operating Instructions for the Still ~ 1921

When Lieutenant Lagerstadt moved to the estate and began tinkering with the Still, it quickly became apparent that he was somewhat of a novice. He reached out for assistance from a friend in New Jersey.

His buddy, Charles Burk told him, *"it might be better for you to stay in the Navy and let Lamesure unto itself."* Nevertheless, he sent him detailed instructions on its proper usage and temperatures, including:

"I suggest that you open an account with a US National Bank in San Juan and get a $5,000 to $10,000 line of credit, otherwise you will shortly be at the mercy of the St. Thomas pirates and likely get fleeced out of your investment.

"Buy your supplies in Puerto Rico or the States.

"Get Lieutenant Evans to show you how to connect the Still to a Steam Still. This will enable you to control distillation and enable you to make 3 or 4 fractions or grades of oil.

"For fine grades, improve your cooling or condensing systems and stop all leaks between the Still and the condenser.

"The fine oil is highly volatile! Get a good thermometer and place the bulb inside the top of the Still above the waterline.

"The scale outside the Still should read 250° F and the visible part of the scale should include about 100°F or from 150° to 250° F.

"Never have the water line higher than the middle of the still, otherwise, you will drive over water and lose oil, as you can't separate the property without a centrifuge.

"Best get a chopper and chop up leaves as fresh as you can get them. Then cook them up first in freshwater, to which add salt after first or second fractions in increasing amounts, to saturation or better, anywhere up to twenty percent.

"This will salt out the oil to the surface and increase the boiling point, getting you all the low grades. If you want the Bay water too, you'll probably have to fire up above 212° F.

"You may want to purchase some books on the subject……"

The Lamesure Estate house © Creque Family Archives

Bay Oil Distribution

After many attempts, the Lieutenant eventually felt comfortable working with the Still and produced a quantity of bay oil.

He followed his friend's advice and sought distribution through the firm of *Magnus, Mabee & Reynard, Inc.* in New York. They were interested in receiving the full particulars regarding price, quantity, and consignments, being both manufacturers and importers of essential oils.

"Relative to Citric Acid, we are also very much interested in this. I would be pleased to have you favor us with full particulars as promptly as possible," said PC Magnus, the company's President.

Listing Lamesure For Sale ~ 1922

For unknown reasons, Lieutenant Lagerstadt decided to sell the estates after owning them for about a year. Interestingly, it was the property's former owner, Mrs. Westbrook, who placed the advertisement. She described the estates as the '*most romantic*' she had ever seen.

The Beauty of Bordeaux Mountain 1922

The sprawling panorama of *Lamesure* and *Bordeaux Mountain,* when viewed from the sea, was vast and breathtaking!

From the crystal-blue beach below, the land rose up along several knolls and valleys to reach a 1,200-foot pinnacle. The view from the crest spanned across Flanagan Island to the British Virgins, including Norman Island and Pelican Island.

Herman was so impressed by its beauty that he purchased the estates from the Lagerstadt family without any hesitation.

A Serene Retreat with 1,400+ Acres

Included were 1,400 acres with 100 head of cattle, horses, mules, goats, several bathing beaches, excellent fishing banks with hundreds of hardwood trees and bay leaf trees surrounding the house.

The principal bay was deep enough of an anchorage to hold several large vessels.

All the machinery, equipment, boats, tackle, household furniture, and furnishings accompanied the sale.

Herman had been looking for a beautiful, serene retreat after suddenly losing both his parents. They died of natural causes within six months of each other. *Lamesure* was the paradise he sought, and he hoped the move from Hassel Island would be the change his family needed.

Herman and Emily Creque © The author's great-grandparents, Creque Family Archives

The view from Bordeaux Mountain © Creque Family Archives

The advertisement described the soil as *'well adapted for the raising of limes and coconuts'*, of which there were several large groves.

Herman thought it would be a good idea to develop this to its fullest extent and expended considerable sums of money. He would also specialize in the raising and selling of cattle and mules.

He assumed the balance of the Lagerstadt's mortgage, $13,500, and reportedly paid $15,000 for the estates in total on May 8, 1922.

Exactly five years had passed since the islands had been ceded to the United States, and they were now under American rule.

When the editor at the local newspaper heard the property had been purchased by a local businessman, he complimented Herman, *our enterprising citizen*, on his latest business venture, and wished him *a full measure of success.*

The Bordeaux Bay Trees

At the time, fifty acres of the lofty hillsides were covered in bay trees, however, due to the severity of the drought, the crop was in '*the worst possible condition.'* Not the type to sit around idly,

Herman began making improvements. Almost immediately, he spent:

- $1500 in new barbed wire fencing
- 200 acres in grass and 400 acres with bay tree seedlings.

The History of Bay Rum

The Bayberry, or Pimenta Acris, yielded a leaf and berry out of which a superior bay rum was manufactured and exported all over the world. It was said that *'no other place in the world produced so fine a berry and leaf for this business as the St. John Bay tree.'*

According to an article written in 1912, it was believed the island of St. Kitts was the birthplace of bay rum.

It reported that *'around 1872, Old Mrs. French of St. Kitts was the first maker of bay rum or bay water as it was then called.*

In 1921, when the *Willis-Campbell Act* was passed in the United States, it extended prohibition to the Virgin Islands, making the manufacture and distribution of bay rum forbidden in the territory.

Therapeutic Uses of Bay Oil

Bay rum, however, had been used in the islands for many years for its therapeutic properties. It was preferred mostly as a body rub for colds and muscle pains and the treatment of rheumatism and circulation problems. By warming the oil, it could also be used as part of aromatherapy to help the respiratory and digestive systems.

Since a license was needed to operate a still during these censured times, Herman applied and was granted a license under Title II of the National Prohibition Act. ~ *1927*

Extracting the Bay Oil

The extraction process was quite straightforward. With the proper knowledge regarding the correct boiling temperatures, one could produce a high-quality product.

When the trees were mature and the leaves collected, they were brought to the still-house near the beach for boiling, but sometimes, bags of leaves were sent directly to St. Thomas, where they were processed and infused with alcohol and water at the rear of A.H. Riise's store.

The firm of A.H. Riise © The Royal Library of Denmark

A Comparison of Bay Rums ~ 1888

The firm of A.H. Riise's in St. Thomas made one of the most popular bay rums on the island, having won many prizes.

There was an interesting comparison of the product by a visitor to the islands. James T. Shinn compared the Bay Spirit distilled by A.H. Riise with other commercial varieties of imported bay rum and found A.H. Riise's product *'the most agreeable and refreshing of any.'*

Those he tested varied in alcoholic strength ranging from forty to forty-eight percent by weight of alcohol, and in color and odor. A.H. Riise's was nearly white and strong in spirit, while the odor was more fragrant and lasting than any of the others examined. It had the aromatic fragrance of the real bay leaf, which may be owed to it being distilled by steam from the selected fresh leaves of a genuine bay tree.

The Popularity of Bay Rum ~ 1899

It was once asserted, on the best authority, that the President-Elect of the Great United States of America, Ben Harrison, used bay rum that originated from St. Thomas on his hair.

Even the Romans loved the bay tree! They believed that the sweet, fresh, spicy scent of the bay oil herb was symbolic of *wisdom, peace, and protection.*

The Bay Leaf Christmas Tree ~ 1899

Years ago, the bay tree was known as the Christmas tree. This was because it was in *'a perfect state of bloom'* during the holiday season. All the churches used it for their holiday decorations.

'When the branches were taken down after New Year's Day, they were not thrown away, but carefully preserved and used, much like cinnamon is today.'

Drinking Bay Rum Could Be Deadly!

Drinking the bay rum mixture was disastrous! Considering the possible consequences and detrimental effects, several people attempted despite the product's warnings that it was for *external use* only.

Operating the still © The Royal Library of Denmark, Tyge Hvass Collection

In 1911, there was a violent disturbance on the steamer, *Canadia* when the crew attacked the captain for no reason! The trouble was said to have been caused by the men being drunk from drinking bay rum.

"*One man had to be knocked down and put into irons and five were arrested and brought ashore to prison to await trial.*"

On the British steamer, *Thimbleby*, it was deadly! *'It cost the life of one man and set the others to fighting amongst themselves after a free inward use of the product had been made.'*

This news was disconcerting, and port officials worried that trade with St. Thomas might slow with captains *'fearing trouble, delay, and expense.'* A ban was placed temporarily on the selling of bay rum directly to the boats in the harbor, but it continued to be a popular product despite the surrounding controversy over its ingestion.

The Aromatic Bay Leaves

Within a couple of years of caring for and nurturing the crop at *Bordeaux*, the new bay trees planted had grown over twelve feet high. The hillsides were beautiful once again, with the verdant blooms of aromatic leaves.

An Award-Winning Product

Bay rum was an award-winning export wherever it was exhibited. With its pungent and distinctive odor, it consistently received the highest accolades possible, over all its competitors.

Unfortunately, the bay tree is no longer harvested commercially, and as of 1947, was "almost extinct." In 1962, the *Virgin Islands Daily News* gave the reason why this was so.

It was due to the *'lack of pickers and the dying out of the bay tree. This forced companies to seek bay oil elsewhere.'*

Today, the *St. Johns Fragrance Company* in St. Thomas sells a range of bay rum products with imported oils. They include scented soaps, aftershave, moisturizers, candles, and their classic signature cologne.

In 2017, the company celebrated its 70th anniversary.

AH Riise Bay Rum © Viggo Molle

The Governor Visits ~ 1922

Proud to see his bay crop doing so well, Herman took every opportunity to show local authorities the progress he was making. He'd been caring for the orchards for five months and was seeing marked improvements.

Governor Henry Hough
© history.navy.mil

While casually glancing through the newspapers one day, he learned that a party of dignitaries was planning an official inspection visit of all schools in Cruz Bay and Coral Bay.

He thought this would be an ideal opportunity to invite the governor and very likely sent him a formal invitation.

One of the fastest boats stationed in the islands was chartered to transport the officials. Herman knew of the boat's reputation, having met the Captain when it was serviced at the railway.

Although it's uncertain whether the dignitaries had time to visit, it was very probable, as *'Governor Hough was known to give serious attention to the island's concerns. He was a man of marked ability, sympathy, and understanding.'*

Historic Fire Destroys Sub-Chaser ~ 1923

The following year, there was a terrible accident involving this Submarine Chaser that the Governor used to visit the out-islands.

The *SC-340* was thought to be indestructible since it was a staunch seagoing vessel, but one day, it suddenly caught fire and sank. It happened when a group of visitors were leaving the Cruz Bay wharf, heading back to St. Thomas.

SC 340/Submarine Chaser at the Creque Marine Railway © Valerie Sims

Luckily, the accident occurred close enough to shore so that the passengers and crew could be safely rescued. The Governor quickly dispatched the *USS Grebe* to transport everyone back to St. Thomas.

This historic fire, among others around the United States, was classified as *'one of the key events that significantly shaped today's International Fire and Life Safety Codes'* regarding boat safety. Further details of what triggered the fire were never published in the newspaper.

A Survey Near Estate Carolina ~ 1923

Among Herman's papers was a handwritten note with a notation of a plot he had surveyed near *Estate Carolina*. He hired Dante Beretta and Mr. Moron of St. Thomas to survey the land, but its exact location is uncertain, perhaps *5F Bordeaux*. (February 2, 1923)

This is an interesting account of how properties were surveyed using trees, gates, and roads as boundary posts. His notes read:

'Measure off the 4 acres belonging to (name unclear), the boundary on the 4 acres bought by me (Herman O. Creque) from JP Jorgensen, formerly owned by Edwin Testamark.

'The boundary line of four acres is as follows:

- *Beginning from the boundary post in the road by the huts near Carolina, to around the turn in a southerly direction and westerly to the gate.*
- *Go 273 feet from the gate, going northwest, meeting a Mango tree and a Plumtree 272 feet from the gate.*

Surveying land on St. John © Valerie Sims, Creque Family Archives

- *Continuing along the track road to a Plumtree.*
- *Go 805 feet, thence, east up the hill to a boundary post on top of the hill.*
- *Go 287 feet, thence, in a southeast direction to a boundary post in the road from which we started, 592 feet.'*

When drawn, this property was shaped like a rectangle. Given the above, it's no wonder there are so many land disputes over boundary lines today!

Emily and her youngest daughter, 4-year old Margie, 1923 © Creque Family Archives

Lounging at the Lamesure Home ~ 1923

While Herman focused on improvements around the estate, his wife appreciated the comforting amenities of a well-appointed home, wanting it to feel warm and inviting.

Since it was already partially furnished, Emily, my great-grandmother brought special keepsakes that would personalize the rooms, like photographs of her family, books, statues, and a phonograph music player for enjoyment.

Emily's Family

Emily descended from a large family in St. Thomas that immigrated to the island from Spain during the eighteenth century. Her father owned and operated a bakery in his name, the *Manuel Cid Bakery,* established around 1866.

In 1912, the name was changed to the *Naval Bakery* before being sold to the *St. Thomas Steam Bakery Ltd.* During its early years, the business was successful and afforded Emily and her siblings a quality education. She attended Queens College in Barbados and later, a Catholic college in Trinidad. It's probably where her love of books began.

Emily's Favorite Collections

Now that she was going to be spending more time on St. John, she brought to the house as many of her prized assortment of hard-covered collections as she could. With Tardy's help, they neatly arranged them in the bookshelves that hugged the walls.

As an avid reader, Emily spent many hours in her rocking chair, escaping to faraway lands, whenever she had the opportunity. Popular novels in the 1920s were *The Velveteen Rabbit*, *Siddhartha* and, *The Curious Case of Benjamin Button.* Perhaps one of these was enjoyed, but her known favorite was her Bible.

As a devout Catholic, Emily was responsible for helping to convert her husband to Catholicism. Her love for her God and belief in Christianity was a devotion she and Tardy shared.

Tardy's Helping Hands, 1903 – 1980

Tardy was the family's beloved nanny and cook for five generations! Her full name was Thelma Eliza Meyers. She helped Emily with everything and very likely was the one who packed all the necessary items for the move. In 1922, they maintained homes on Hassel Island and Main Street in St. Thomas.

Born in 1903 during the Danish times, Tardy moved in with the family when she was fourteen years old and became a permanent member, loved and adored by everyone.

Thelma (Tardy) Meyers May 9, 1903 ~ May 4, 1980 © Creque Family Archives

No one knew what had become of her parents since she was so young, but she helped with running the household, cooking and caring for the children, and keeping the home tidy.

She never married or showed any interest in anyone or anything other than her Church and her beloved Bible.

Tardy cared for Emily when she was ailing, watched over her children, grandchildren, and great-grandchildren (when they went to her house after school), and cuddled Emily's first great-great-granddaughter, Anika, during her senior years.

Tardy loved them all and sent birthday, graduation cards, and rosaries wishing them all of God's blessings, even when they became adults.

Despite her gentle nature though, she had moments when she took a no-nonsense approach and was quite strict. According to my grandmother, when she and her brothers misbehaved, Tardy locked them all up in the chicken coop!

Lunchtime at Lamesure

Emily loved to entertain and often invited her lady friends for tea and lunch, the largest meal of the day. According to Marion, her first grandchild, Tardy served various soups before the main meal.

My mother remembered the delicious pumpkin soups, chicken soups, and bean soups like red, split pea, and black-eyed pea soups she offered guests in her Main Street home.

Food was freshly caught and on any given occasion, fish, conch, lobster, beef, or venison was served. Other specialties included Shepherd's Pie, a stuffed eggplant called *Berenjena*, stewed or boiled saltfish, smoked oyster pie, and sautéed meatballs.

The view of Lamesure Bay © Creque Family Archives

Marion's husband, Richard fondly remembered when he helped himself to *three* meatballs one day, Tardy was not happy and gently slapped his hand, conveying her message that *two* were sufficient. After all, her domain was the kitchen; even if Madam ruled the house, Tardy had the last say at mealtimes.

One of the desserts she loved to make was a creamy custard with a sweet strawberry topping, but there were many more just as scrumptious.

Light beverages she served could be pineappleade, Maubi, lemonade, or a soursop juice prepared by removing the seeds and stem and blending it with water, sweetened condensed milk, and fresh, grated nutmeg.

Tardy's meals were always delicious. She had a natural gift to turn anything she prepared into the most sumptuous of experiences.

As kids, we used to argue over which cup we used to enjoy her homemade cocoa. It still brings back the fondest memories for me. The red cowboy boot cup or the yellow? Either way, the contents were yummy!

Lunch was the largest and most popular meal of the day, with many guests and family members casually stopping by, knowing they were in for a sumptuous feast.

While life at *Lamesure Estate* was much more reclusive and quieter than St. Thomas, one or more of these lunch specialties would very likely be prepared, as Tardy traveled with her copybook—filled with her recipes—everywhere she went.

Devoted to her Catholic Church

In St. Thomas, the family attended the Sts. Peter and Paul Catholic Church, sitting in the second pew on the right-hand side. It was reserved in their name, and only immediate family members were allowed to be there.

In those days, pews were rented and on occasion, Emily politely reminded those unaware of the arrangement that this was their private seating area.

At home, her assortment of religious statues adorned almost every room. Diane, her granddaughter, remembered the statues of the *Sacred Heart* and the *Mother of Perpetual Help*, to whom she prayed for guidance. They were a great comfort for her, placed on an altar she had built for this purpose.

Collecting Fine China ~ 1935

One of Emily's pleasing pastimes was collecting fine china, including beautiful figurines and dolls. When the *Maison Danoise Shop* opened in St. Thomas, it became her favorite store, with many of her keepsakes purchased there.

Porcelain Piano Babies

Emily admired the delicate, porcelain piano babies they offered in various sizes. They made the perfect adornment for her piano in her Main Street home, keeping the light shawl that draped across the top from slipping.

These miniature dolls were one of the most endearing relics of the Victorian era.
A few years ago, my mother visited her cousin, Mary Alice, who inherited one of her grandmother's piano babies.

Seeing and holding the doll again brought back a feeling of love and joy, both for her grandmother and her memorable childhood.

Treasured Gifts

Emily wrapped and gifted many souvenirs from this little French shop. One special present she gave was a complete set of blue cornflower china in the Demeter pattern, made by Bing and Grøndahl in Denmark.

My mother was the lucky recipient on her wedding day.

Emily's love was magnanimous, and today, this treasured gift has passed to the next generation, together with the story of how it came to be in the family.

Demeter pattern, made in Denmark

Emily Beatrice Cid-Creque © Valerie Sims, Creque Family Archives

Emily and Margie who was born on Hassel Island in 1919 © Creque Family Archives

The Tea Pot Collection

From old photographs, it's evident that Emily's delicate teapot collection had been brought to *Lamesure* as well. They were displayed, together with the sugar bowls and creamers, in the sitting room on a narrow shelf above a heavy mirror.

One would think this was unsuitable given the numerous tremors the islands experienced from time to time. Besides, with five children in the home, one slam of the door would send them all crashing down to the floor.

Perhaps this was a room Emily enjoyed quietly to herself. Tardy would have made sure that all the children stayed out.

Emily's Generosity

Despite her strict reputation as the *Lady of the House*, Emily was exceedingly generous and had a soft heart. Besides her family, she gave money, gifts, and baked goods to those in need.

Every year as the holidays approached, she made fruit cakes as presents for those less fortunate. It was an annual Christmas tradition that her father started when he distributed food, pastries, and cakes for the poor.

Interestingly, Manuel V. Cid fed many of the families displaced during the *St. Croix Labor Riot of 1878,* when they traveled to St. Thomas for assistance. For twenty-six days straight, he baked 100 loaves of bread every day and distributed them at no cost.

Baking Sweet Breads

Now, Tardy, with her assistant, was preparing to do the same and mixed all the dough by hand.

Everyone looked forward to the finished loaves with great anticipation. When baked, she laid them out on platters on a huge table in the parlor, waiting for them to cool.

The whole family loved the deep, rich aroma of roasted cinnamon and French vanilla essence that permeated the rooms. These delicious fruitcakes were shared with St. John families as well as the Frenchtown community of St. Thomas.

Emily's legacy most certainly lives on in the hearts of those she helped.

(One of the family's traditional fruitcake recipes is available in the bonus section. Visit, VintageStJohnBook.com/bonus.)

Celebrating July 4th in Coral Bay ~ 1923

A year after settling into the neighborhood, one of the earliest gatherings to honor the US Independence Day celebrations took place in Coral Bay.

The church bells *'rang out wildly'* at Emmaus and awakened the community for the organized activities. Herman was on the Executive Committee and helped plan the scheduled sailing regatta.

Emmaus Moravian Church, Coral Bay, St. John © A Postcard

As everyone gathered at the shoreline, the sloops prepared for one of '*the largest and most imposing'* races ever held on the island.

It was a *'pleasing and entertaining spectacle'* as thirteen boats entered to participate.

The Sailboat Race

The course extended from the bay in Saunders Gut, eastward around Norman Island, and back to Penn's Point in *Little Plantation*. The two judges, Carl E. Francis, and Sebastien Lefee gave the signal for the start.

With the next strong puff of wind, the boats filled their sails and advanced their way toward the horizon. Anxious eyes followed them until they were lost behind Norman Island.

The wait seemed to take forever, before suddenly, without warning, a shout went around that they were coming back!

As the boats raced across the finishing line, onlookers clapped and cheered for the winning vessel. It was a very exciting moment for the spectators!

Reverend G.F. Penn at the Reef Bay Petroglyphs © The Maritime Museum of Denmark

The Winners

The winner was *West India,* captained by veteran boat-builder, Alphonso Roberts of East End. Captain Lewis Sprauve of Cruz Bay was especially pleased because he was the owner of the winning boat.

Next came *India,* captained by Benjamin O'Neal of East End, and third, the *Triumph,* captained by Arnold Hendricks of Saunders Gut. Arnold had lost his previous boat in the hurricane of 1916, and the *Triumph* was his new vessel.

With the *'battle in the sea'* over, the captains and crews assembled into the big hall of the parsonage. Reverend and Mrs. G.F. Penn took pleasure in serving dinner and refreshments as Carl Francis complimented the participants. He praised them for their *'spirit of manly rivalry'* and consoled those who *'fell short of victory.'*

The Prizes

Mrs. Penn distributed the prizes to the grateful winners:

- First Prize: Lewis Sprauve, *West India - $8.00*
- Second Prize: Benjamin O'Neal, *India - $5.00*
- Third Prize: Arnold Hendricks, *Triumph - $3.00*

A silver cup was presented to Captain Sprauve, which he was allowed to keep so long as he maintained the lead every year.

The day was a joyous one and the occasion would not have been a success without the support of the Reverend and his wife. Widespread gratitude was extended to them for their interest and devotion.

Unfortunately, the happy times did not last long. The following summer, another deadly and destructive hurricane hit the island that would destroy many of the boats.

This was heartbreaking, especially for Reverend Penn who lost everything in the Hurricane of 1916, including his valuable books.

A view of Cruz Bay, St. John, Danish West Indies © The Royal Library of Denmark

St. John Hit Hard by Hurricane ~ 1924

When panicked radio messages were received from Antigua and later St. Kitts, officials knew trouble was heading their way again!

They couldn't believe it! Acting on the information quickly, two red flags were hoisted at the signal stations on all three islands. At midday, two guns were fired, one immediately after the other. After an intermission of half a minute, two more guns were fired, warning everybody of the approaching storm.

Windows were closed and preparations were immediately underway. It was *'a race against the clock,* and *the sound of the hammer could be heard in all directions!'*

The weather was cloudy and sultry at first, but the barometer stayed steady. Then, from seven in the evening, the wind began to blow heavily in gusts. It increased in force and velocity until three in the morning, when it gradually subsided.

The more powerful gusts came from the northwest and appeared to be the worst. They did the greatest damage to St. John and Tortola. This disaster killed at least eight inhabitants on St. John and wounded more than nine, according to the first reports. Those that perished during the storm were:

- James Matthias Sr. of *Estate Mandahl* in East End
- Winfield Matthias
- Mathew George at *Johns Folly*
- Alfred Lambertis, his wife and child
- Idalia Blake
- Cyril Blake
- Mary Matthias
- Adalia Matthias and her infant son at *Estate Hermitage.*
- John Testamark was missing; last seen at *Estate Carolina.*

The wounded were: Ernest Wells, Rudolf Benjamin, Wilfred Wells, James Mathias, Alfred Mathias, Lancy Wiltshire, Felix Biel, Roslyn Fraser, Eva George, Alfred Jackson, Rudolph Anduze, Carolina Daniel, Carmelita Joseph, Estelle George and Dr. Palmer.

Governor Phillip Williams sent the *USS Grebe* over to bring tents and provisions for Coral Bay, Cruz Bay, and Francis Bay.

When the ship returned, they reported that the damage to St. John was *more severe* than the rest of the islands. Besides the recorded deaths, houses and boats were demolished, the bay rum factory was gone, and numerous cattle were found floating in the bay.

Hurricane Losses

Many lost everything they owned, including their small, cultivated gardens. Without these resources, they could no longer buy or trade for their necessary provisions, including bread, sugar, flour, rice, cornmeal, peas, butter and salt fish.

Messages of Sympathy

Messages of sympathy came in from the US President and the Acting Secretary of the Navy.

"I am deeply distressed to hear of the tragedy that has befallen the people of the Virgin Islands.

Will you convey to them my sincerest sympathy, particularly to the bereaved relatives of those who have been killed." (President Calvin Coolidge, September 2, 1924)

A radiogram from the Acting Secretary of the Navy: *"Shocked to hear of the tragedy that has befallen the people of the Virgin Islands. I am sure you are taking all measures possible to alleviate distress. Convey to all, my sincerest sympathy in this time of trouble."* (Theodore Roosevelt, Jr., September 2, 1924)

No one believed another hurricane tragedy would hit the islands so soon after the devastating hurricane of 1916, which was still fresh in their memories.

As resilient as Virgin Islanders were, they began again, the long journey to recovery.

A Special St. John Visitor ~ 1928

Captain Franz Romer in St. Thomas, US Virgin Islands

After four years, the hurricane tragedy was still a painful memory, but residents rebuilt what they could and tried to find a new sense of normalcy in their day to day existence.

When a chance encounter brought an unexpected foreigner to their shores, the community warmly embraced him.

Captain Franz Romer, 1899 – 1928 © Creque Family Archives

Captain Franz Romer ~ 1928

The young sea traveler was German-born, Franz Romer. He quickly became a local hero when residents learned of his daring adventure to cross the Atlantic, alone in a 21-foot sea kayak.

Many were amazed by his fortitude and courage.

Romer was very ambitious. When he learned of Charles Lindbergh's financial success and notoriety after flying across the Atlantic in the *Spirit of St. Louis,* he had hopes of setting a world record of his own. A prize of $25,000 awaited him in New York if his daring adventure was successful.

The Captain's Crossing

The weary Captain had a difficult and tumultuous crossing that first began in Lisbon, Portugal. When he stopped in St. Thomas for rest and supplies, he had been crouched in his canoe for fifty-eight, continuous days, traversing over 3,000 miles in this position.

Dangerously rough seas, high winds, and physical exhaustion almost consumed him. When he disembarked, he was unable to stand or fully stretch out his legs.

Herman's private balcony in St. Thomas with his mounted binoculars © Creque Family Archives

Meeting the Captain

During his stay, the twenty-nine-year-old met many acquaintances who became extremely fond and enamored with him. Both Herman and his fifteen-year-old son, Henry were thrilled to befriend him.

In St. Thomas, there was a wooden jetty that Herman owned, extending into the harbor very close to where the Captain may have anchored. It was used for deliveries and supplies for his hardware store whenever they landed by boat. He likely met the Captain on the dock when he arrived in the early morning hours of August 1.

If not there, then he most probably spotted him from his balcony on the upper floor room, above his childhood home on the warehouse rooftop. This was his private study where he listened to the BBC news and kept an eye on his wall-mounted barometer in case of impending bad weather.

As a member of the Harbor Board since 1923, Herman used this perch to keep a vigilant lookout to the sea below with his outdoor binoculars, which were mounted on the railing.

A Visit to St. John ~ 1928

Unfortunately, Romer's harrowing ordeal left him suffering from scars and painful burns from sun exposure and sea spray. He needed rest before he could continue on the last leg of his journey.

Herman was kind and offered him his home at *Lamesure* to recuperate. There, Romer planned to stay about a month.

He would order a couple of outboard motors from Germany to assist him in case of bad weather since it was late summer, and the hurricane season was in full swing. The weeks it would take for them to arrive would give him the needed time to regain his health.

Finding a Photograph

A surprise find in the family album was a photograph of Romer standing below a shaded tree near the livestock pens. His pronounced jawline and deep-set eyes were impossible to miss.

Tucked snugly under his left arm was a leather pouch that very likely contained his log journals, detailing the events of his journey. I wondered what they revealed about what happened to him in the middle of the Atlantic Ocean?

When I read through the old newspapers hoping to learn more, it was there that I discovered that sharks had bumped his kayak and the twist of their fins almost ripped the soft bottom open. Wasn't he afraid? The newspapers reported that he couldn't swim! Several steamers stopped to assist him, but he refused their rescue attempts.

Long Talks at Lamesure

I imagined the animated conversations the family must have had around the dining table. The Captain's English was limited, but those he met said he had no trouble communicating.

Henry probably asked him a million questions, especially about the size of the waves or about his shark encounters.

He was fascinated by marine life, ever since he caught a strange type of fish that crawled on the seabed floor. No one had ever seen one in the islands before, and it turned out to be a rare type of batfish.

Henry also witnessed one of the most dangerous sharks ever caught in St. Thomas, a Great White! As a nine-year-old, he never forgot that exciting moment when it was pulled from the waters near Hassel Island. Everyone talked about it for weeks.

The Blood-Curdling Moments

Unfortunately, the Captain kept many of the details of his trip to himself, hoping one day to write a book about his experiences.

He was very secretive, but he did make an insightful remark to someone, hinting at the *'heartbreaking and blood-curdling moments'* he experienced as he crossed the Atlantic.

Captain Romer riding in a new Cadillac in the parade © Creque Family Archives

The Honorary Parade ~ Aug 22, 1928

When he recovered, Romer was celebrated as a hero for his survival, and an official reception was organized. The governor honored him by showering him with accolades for his bravery and a gold medal was commissioned from the local firm of F.M. Corneiro as a symbol of his brilliant achievement.

The Golden Gift

Engraved on the disc were his initials, *F* and *R*, along with an image of his kayak and the words, ★ *For Merit* ★ *Lisbon – St. Thomas.*

A special holiday was chosen for a grand parade and when the day arrived, thousands lined the roadways to catch a glimpse of this young explorer. Seated with him in a new Cadillac was Governor Waldo Evans, as well as the President of the Chamber of Commerce, Emile Berne, along with Herman and his son.

Romer's prized kayak was mounted onto a Ford Lory and towed behind the parade route so that everyone could see how small it was. Old Glory flew from her bow, as the Captain's home flag flew from her stern. As soon as the parade participants arrived at the Emancipation Garden, the *'golden gift'* from the people of St. Thomas was presented to him.

Romer was genuinely moved by the Governor's kind words and the generous present he received. He thanked them all for the *'worthy recognition and genial hospitality',* expressing his sincerest gratitude from the bottom of his heart.

Captain Franz Romer departing for San Juan © Courtesy of Ronald Lockhart

Paddling to Puerto Rico ~ August 24, 1928

A couple of days after the public parade, it was time for Romer to continue on his journey to New York. There were still many stops to make along the route before arriving at his final destination. The Governor wished the brave Captain *farewell* and *Godspeed* as he embarked on the next leg of his journey.

When Romer paddled away from King's Wharf, he headed west into the sunset, unaware of the frightful danger he would later face.

After his departure, Herman and Henry followed him on the *s/s Catherine*, sailing to Puerto Rico on the same day.

It's uncertain whether Romer invited them to join him in the San Juan celebrations or they were simply star-struck by their famous guest, but both of their names were found on the ship's manifest.

Captain Franz Romer

It took Romer twenty-four hours paddling and sailing to reach San Juan harbor and when he arrived, he received a joyous reception as anticipated. He stayed in Puerto Rico for seventeen days. Why so long? We may never know. He was fully stocked and well-rested while in St. Thomas.

The Captain's Fate

Whatever the reason for his prolonged departure, it had dire consequences. After leaving San Juan on September 11, hurricane warnings were received by the weather station there, but unfortunately, it was impossible to transmit those warnings to Romer. He was likely sailing off the eastern tip of the Dominican Republic by then.

When the heavy rains began, Herman said a silent prayer, hoping his new friend was able to pull into a safe harbor. Unbeknownst to him, his worst fears were later confirmed. The Captain was never heard from again since that fateful September day.

Hurricane Damage ~ 1928

On their arrival back at *Lamesure*, it was evident that their home had sustained significant damage. This was worrisome because Herman did not expect the storm to be as destructive as it was.

With thoughts of Captain Romer on his mind, he had to turn his attention back to repairing the house.

Unfortunately, the entire roof was ripped off and needed replacement, a cost of $180 according to the surveyor.

Donald S. Boreham, an assistant to the Public Works Officer at St. Thomas, examined the damage in early October.

'The home's flooring was all warped and buckled and the interior decoration spoiled by water.' All had to be replaced for $210.

Mr. Boreham apologized for the delay in the execution of the survey, as it was *'difficult to obtain transportation due to the shortage of motorboats following the storm.'* (Sept 13, 1928)

Campaigning on the Blue Ticket ~ 1932

With the hope of improving the economic conditions of the islands, Herman joined the *Blue Team* and campaigned for a coveted seat on the Colonial Council to represent St. John.

He was one of *'six capable and efficient men'* willing and able to work for the salvation of the islands.

Accompanying him on the Blue Ticket were Herbert E. Lockhart, Donald S. Boreham, Cyril V. Francois, D. Victor Bornn and Dr. V.A. Christensen.

Voting Day at Fort Christian © Creque Family Archives

In the interests of improving the island and its infrastructure, they promised to address the development of the St. Thomas harbor, improve the roads, and develop tourist attractions and facilities for the accommodation of winter visitors.

There would be a moratorium on unpaid taxes due before 1931, and they planned to establish a suitable banking institution to take the place of the National Bank of the Danish West Indies.

Also, on their radar, was to create new industries that would furnish employment and promote vocational training, as well as expand the Homestead Plan for both St. Thomas and St. John.

Victory!

Happily, they beat the Red and the White team to take the victory!

Despite the impending weather, a handful of St. John voters *'stumbled through the weather-beaten, narrow trails to cast their vote, and for once, air themselves on issues that annoyed them.'*

Working men wore different shades of blue shirts and even the policemen wore blue flannels under their khaki uniforms.

It was self-evident that St. John went *Blue!* Herman stood without opposition and took the island by unanimous vote, fifteen. His constituents guaranteed that they would leave no stone unturned in seeking to promote the welfare of the islands. They put up a hard fight to win the campaign, promising to stand for *'dignity and progress.'*

Their success, in part, may have been attributed to this popular slogan, which they promoted in *The Virgin Islands Daily News,* October 1932:

It's up to you to be true, vote for Blue!

The True Blue Ticket
For Town:
Herbert E. Lockhart
Donald S. Boreham
Cyril V. Francois
D. Victor Bornn
For Country:
Dr. V. A. Christensen
For St. John:
Herman O. Creque

The cattle at Lamesure Estate © Creque Family Archives

Clearing Cabritte Horn ~ 1934

Victorious in his quest for a seat in the Colonial Council, Honorable Creque, as he was referred to in his new capacity, turned his attention to expanding the livestock business. It kept him and the laborers he hired very busy.

During the 1930s and 1940s, the workers cleared eighty-five acres of *Cabritte Horn* for additional livestock pens, installing hundreds of wooden stakes that held the attached barbed-wire fencing in place. Several of the hired hands lived nearby: John Prince, Alfred George, Waldermar "Wally" Jackson, Sanford Myers, Nathaniel Thomas, Lancy Wilshire, Charles Bastian, and Mr. Mathias.

A Cattle and Horse-Raising Island

Raising cattle was an important industry for the meat, milk and other products it produced. St. John, after all, was known as a *'cattle and horse-raising island',* and evidence of this was found on the roads. Everywhere one walked was marked by the droppings from these animals!

Livestock at Lamesure Estate © Valerie Sims, Creque Family Archives

Leading the Herd

Every evening, the herd was led down from the hillsides to be watered and returned to the safety of their pens. Their deep bellows reverberated for miles over the hills, signaling the end of another lazy, grazing day.

Every color was represented, with some animals being light-brown, others black, brown or tawny in appearance. Some were very thin and emaciated, despite how much they consumed.

As they trotted along past the shoreline, the workers cracked their whips in the air, pushing them to move along. A few cows swung their tails nervously back and forth as others kicked up their hind legs in agitation.

The smaller calves tended to linger and frolic along the water's edge, slowing down the herd. When their mothers heard them from the nearby pens, they called to them anxiously with louder bellows. It was a noisy cacophony of farm sounds when all the animals knew it was feeding time.

Milking the Cows

The cows were milked at the end of the day to produce a higher yield, and sometimes, it was not always easy to get the milk from the cows.

To facilitate the process, some of the calves were separated from their mothers early in the morning to prevent them from suckling. When they were reunited, they were allowed to suckle for a few minutes to bring down the milk. Ordinarily, the cows and calves were kept together the whole day. This made for the happiest and fattest calves.

Riding the Cows

The worker's young sons helped considerably with the livestock and were an asset to the business. At times, they were sometimes mischievous and as opportunities presented themselves for some fun, the boys didn't hesitate to seize the moment. When no one was looking, one or more of them attempted to ride the cows around the pen.

They figured out a way to keep a cow from side-stepping while they mounted. If a small rag was twisted around her horns, she stayed still, thinking she was tied. As one of the boys jumped on her back, a quick, bumpy trot was enough of a break before he quickly dismounted in laughter. Those playful moments of escape were fun, but there was another activity they loved even more!

Who Flung Dung?

It was a fun game, similar to one called, *Who Flung Dung?*

Since the huge, dried cow-cakes were everywhere, the boys speared them with sticks and flung them at one another, giggling when they hit their intended targets and broke apart.

Today, cow dung is processed and sold as fertilizer, but back in the day, the excrement was nothing more than an undesirable by-product.

A few of the laborers at Lamesure Estate © Creque Family Archives

Working with the cows was enjoyable, but the hours could be long and the weather, hot. Those moments of laughter released the tension from a workday that ran from dawn to dusk.

The Animal Inventory ~ 1934

The inventory for the estate in June of 1934 consisted of:
82 cows • 30 bulls • 27 steers • 40 heifers • 30 heifer calves and 29 bull calves for a total of 238 animals.

Governor Paul M. Pearson

The Governor Visits ~ 1934

On a beautiful spring day, the family welcomed another distinguished visitor to their home. It was the first civilian governor of the US Virgin Islands, Dr. Paul Martin Pearson. It wasn't the Governor's first visit to the island; that occurred shortly after his inauguration in 1931.

Herman invited him to have a look at the new seedlings he was growing, as well as those planted twelve years prior. He was making significant progress toward a successful harvest and wanted him to see it for himself.

As they saddled up together for the tour of *Bordeaux Mountain*, there was a narrow track crisscrossing the hillsides which the horses knew by heart. When they loosened the reins, the horses continued on their familiar tract. It was an enjoyable outing ascending the steep hillsides together, discussing the advantages and challenges of farming.

Herman O. Creque with his bamboo riding crop © Creque Family Archives

As the two chatted, their bodies swayed back and forth in their saddles, adjusting to the nuances of the rocky path.

Once at the crest, the Governor took a moment to marvel at the expansive view of the harbor from the hilltop. There was no denying how beautiful and captivating the property was.

As he continued through the grove, he was impressed with the progress Herman made and knew it could not have been an easy job given the steep terrain and remote location. The Governor was so moved by *Bordeaux's* beauty and the potential of the bay business, that he recorded his impressions in his diary when he returned home. This sightseeing tour was one of the most memorable experiences of his visit.

Lamesure Estate © Creque Family Archives

Governor Pearson's Diary ~ 1934

Thanks to Governor Pearson's family members, David and Barbara Grove, his diary passage is shared below.

'On Easter Sunday, I went to St. John, direct from St. Thomas harbor to Lameshur Bay. It was just at the foot of Bordeaux Mountain to a 1,200-acre estate owned by H.O. Creque.

On Bordeaux Mountain have grown the best Bay leaves in the world! They are 10% better than any other and produced oil which brought a 10% better price in the world market.

'Our thought is to acquire this property, develop the trees which are now grown any old way, and install a modern still to build up the bay oil business.

'At present, the bay leaf crop is obtained by breaking off the branches from these trees."

'Lameshur is one of the most beautiful estates in the islands!

'The view from Bordeaux Mountain must be one of the most lovely in all the world; sea and clouds and sky, with scores of islands visible from all points of the compass. It was a wonderful day, three hours in the saddle and everything!'

Lamesure Estate © Valerie Sims, Creque Family Archives

The Purchase Offer ~ 1934

A week after the picturesque ride, Herman sent the Governor an interesting letter regarding their earlier conversations. It outlined a sixty-day offer to purchase 501 acres of the property, for $21,500. The breakdown was as follows:

- Fifty acres of bay trees on *Bordeaux Mountain* @ $100 an acre, for $5,000.

- 400 acres of seedling bay trees on *Bordeaux Mountain,* @ $25/acre, for $10,000.

- Fifty acres west of the location of the still on *Lamesure Estate* to mutually agree on @ $60/acre for $3,000.

- The still building on the bay, with one acre surrounding it at $3,500.

Dante Beretta and Mr. Moron of St. Thomas surveyed the land. A note was made that *Mr. Beretta charged $6*, but for unknown reasons, the sale never materialized.

Cruising on the Cheerio ~ 1935

Soon after, everyday affairs turned Herman's attention back to solving problems that popped up.

His sailboat, *Cheerio* needed immediate repairs and was inoperable, probably lying at anchor in *Mary's Creek.* With all his tools and workmen at *Lamesure*, he needed to find a way to get it there.

.

The *Cheerio* was a boat he used to visit Puerto Rico to see the July 4th celebrations or to take sporting fans over to St. Croix to see the horse races. For a group of eighteen or twenty passengers, he charged $2 per person to Christiansted.

According to his advertisements, *'cruising on the Cheerio was not expensive.'* The Braves baseball team once chartered the boat for a tour of St. Croix with fifty fans.

The *Cheerio* in Puerto Rico, July 4, 1932 © Valerie Sims, Creque Family Archives

Luckily, Herman owned another boat, the *J.D. Phillips* which he used to tow the *Cheerio*. It took three hours and twenty-five minutes to get the *Cheerio* to *Lamesure. 'The sea was pretty rough with a good breeze blowing.'*

Towing the Tug

The family had lots of fun excursions on the *J.D. Phillips*. It was the only boat they owned that did not start with the letter "C" for Creque.

Herman purchased this fine motor tugboat to use exclusively as a private pleasure craft. Measuring forty-six feet by ten feet, it was the *'swiftest vessel of her kind in the harbor'*, according to *The Herald* newspaper.

'The J.D. Phillips had the opportunity of demonstrating her qualities when she had a difficult crossing through heavy seas from San Juan via Fajardo. She lost her rudder at sea but was able to make it to Culebra. From there, she was towed to St. Thomas and repaired at the railway.' (*The Herald*, May 31, 1922)

Family fun times on the *J.D. Phillips* © Valerie Sims, Creque Family Archives

Sitting toward the bow of the boat were Herman's wife, Emily, then Margie, her youngest daughter, Frank, Valerie, Henry, and a friend, possibly the daughter of Alan Krigger, who was standing in the water. Mr. Krigger worked for Herman at the railway and also at *Lamesure* and *Annaberg Estate*.

Repairing the Cheerio

As meticulous as Herman was, he made a detailed list of the supplies needed to repair the *Cheerio*.

It wasn't long before the *Cheerio* was available for charters again.

2x6 Pine • 1 Keg nails • Tarp • Deck plugs • Bale of Oakum • One gallon of White paint • Spike bar • Monkey-wrench • Grindstone, 41 pounds of Galvanized nails and a Drill

Fishing to Feed the Family

Fish caught off Lamesure Bay © Creque Family Archives

One of the best fishing grounds near *Lamesure Bay* was just off the beach. John, one of the workmen and his companion caught over fifty fish there in one afternoon!

Not only was fishing a favorite pastime for both Herman and the workmen, but it provided the daily protein requirements needed for a healthy diet.

Chumming the Waters

They chummed the water first to get the best results, then used a light-weighted line with two hooks to catch as many fish as possible.

To make the sand-balls for chumming, John crushed small minnows and sprat and combined them with wet sand, until firm enough to shape into the form of a ball. He then scooped up a generous amount from the bucket, packed it tightly between his hands and shaved off the excess.

As he sat nestled in the corner of his wooden cobble, he threw them overboard one at a time, until the area was well saturated with the odorous mixture. He hoped this would attract the larger fish.

When the sand-balls dissolved, not only did they leave a shimmering, milky trail indicating the current's direction, but they brought the desired fish right to the stern of the boat!

Hauling in the Catch

It wasn't long before John felt the fish nibbling on his bait through the soft skin on the side of his index finger. When a strong enough nibble was felt, he snapped his wrist sharply, snaring his catch!
Hand-over-hand, he pulled the taut line as fast as he could, careful not to get his feet caught in the coiling line, or worse yet, have the line rip through his fingers.

If he wasn't fast enough, he would lose a portion of his catch to a larger fish and end up pulling up only the head. If he was too slow, he would lose the fish altogether.

Experience paid off and it turned into a successful day! The men filled their metal-rimmed buckets with yellowtail snappers, barracudas, parrotfish and more!

When they returned to the bay, they lined their day's catch on the front steps and smiled proudly for a photograph. Everyone looked forward to another deliciously nutritious dinner, as John and his companion were rewarded with a few extra dollars!

Herman Creque under the pergola at Lamesure Estate © Creque Family Archives

The Value of Lamesure Estate ~ 1935

As the summer came to a close, Herman became concerned about the value of his estates after he discovered that a recent appraisal was not as favorable as he believed it should be.

He wrote to the new Commissioner, Dr. Arthur I. Edison, who was the resident medical officer and Government Secretary stationed on St. John.

Herman Creque's Letter to the Commissioner
Aug 31, 1925

'I would have liked to have had a longer chat when you were here last, as I could have explained more in detail the facts about Lamesure.

'I turned up a former appraisal made by Public Works Officer Pettigrew and a member of the Council, Mr. Stakemann, which may be of use to you in determining the valuation.

'I may say that at the time, the estate was in the worst possible condition. Anyone around can testify to that and its subsequent improvement and development.

'At present, we have close to fifty acres in grass alone and the extensive fencing represents an outlay of fifteen hundred dollars.

'From what you said, I gather that the proposed appraisal will fall short of the former valuation. As you mentioned, the dwelling was appraised for $1,500.00, a ridiculous figure. The cistern and pergola alone cost that.

'You will see by the enclosed appraisal that the dwelling was appraised for $6,500.00 by the Public Works officer. Since then, it has been entirely rebuilt exactly as it was before.

'Concerning the land area, we have close to five hundred acres in grass as already stated and fifty acres in bay leaf cultivation that are thirty-five years old. About this, I may say that Mr. Marsh has a similar plot that was recently appraised by Estornel, Bornn, and Bauman at $100.00 per acre.

'There are four hundred acres of bay leaf seedlings, which cannot be classed as Common lands. It only needs to be cleared to produce a bay leaf cultivation as the young trees are already there, the balance is in bushland.'

Mr. Marsh owned:

- 1,238 acres in bushland, appraised at $10/acre.
- 300 acres in grass at $30/acre.
- 40 Acres in bay leaf at $100/acre.

It's evident that cultivating bay leaves increased property values substantially. Herman was justified in being concerned, especially considering the sizable investment he had made since the property's purchase.

An island sloop © Creque Family Archives

The Biggest Sloop Race ~ 1937

As the Thanksgiving holiday was approaching, an exciting sailboat race was organized that brought Herman and the family to East End. Since they loved watching competitive sports, this outing gave everyone a chance to relax and spend some quality time together.

The Course

The course extended from the eastern end of St. John, around Pelican Cay in the British Virgins, and back to East End.

It was a lovely spectacle with fourteen boats representing every neighborhood of the island. Hundreds of spectators watched as a steady procession of open sails danced in the wind.

Preparing the Boats

A week before the race, every boat was on the bay getting their bottoms scraped and a new coat of copper paint. The sails were mended and made as snug as possible, while five or six sandbags replaced much of the ballast.

The Party and Race Winners

People came from everywhere to see the race, traveling by boat, donkey, and horseback. The actual race lasted three and a half hours, but the event lasted a day and a half! There seemed to be no end to the merriment.

Joe Harley's *Vindictive* was the first boat to cross the finish line, fifteen minutes before his competitors. He was closely followed by Charlie Smith's *Arrow* and a few moments later, the *Olive*. Herman knew Charlie personally having purchased a bull from him two years prior.

What a party it was! It ran far into the night with games, a banquet, speeches and lots of cheers for the winner. This was one of the most exciting races the island had ever seen!

The Estate's Profitability

Because large livestock scales were used to weigh each animal sold, Herman knew how much the cattle business earned in revenue. In 1948, for instance, the sale of forty-six cows and thirty-seven goats generated $2,354 in sales.

For the years 1944 to 1948 inclusive, the business earned approximately $16,000 in revenue for the family. The notations for October 1948 were the last entries Herman made in his diary.

The Death of Herman O. Creque, 1884 ~ 1949

Herman passed away unexpectedly, three months later, at age sixty-five after having surgery for appendicitis. ~ *January 29, 1949*

He was one of the island's most prominent businessmen and a former legislator, admired by many. He successfully operated his businesses for more than forty years, including *Creque's Hardware Store* and the *Creque Marine Railway*, up to the time of his retirement.

In his youth, he had been a Cadet in the Home Guard, a Lieutenant in the St. Thomas Militia, then served eight years as a member of the Colonial Council and was a member of the powerful Harbor Board. He was also personally involved with the Red Cross of St. Thomas, the Community Chest, the Chamber of Commerce and—in 1940—was Vice-President of the Cricket Association.

Other involvements included, the 1912 Carnival Committee and the Independence Day Committee, as well as celebrations for the visits of Colonel Charles Lindbergh, the Duke and Duchess of Kent, the Pan American Goodwill Flyers, President Herbert Hoover and Franklin D. Roosevelt among others. Herman loved to be involved in community events and brought his Kodak folding camera to document those rare moments in the island's history.

Herman Creque's Legacy

We're very fortunate that Herman's efforts to develop and cultivate the lands surrounding *Mary's Point* and *Lamesure Estate* were captured in his diary.

Page by page, transactions abounded, with the weights of each cow, the sale of goats and the cost of catching them. Those pencil-written entries brought new life to history.

Herman too, like his father before him, left a fascinating legacy of a time long ago when bay leaf cultivation was considered a viable industry, and cattle was worth their weight in gold.

HERMAN CREQUE

Written by his daughter
© Valerie Creque-Mawson

How we miss you, you will never know.
Ever since we laid you down to rest,
Roving memories of the long ago
Make us think the long past days were best.
And our prayer goes up to God each day;
Near Him, we will keep you while we pray.

Could you only tell us what to do!
Reefs and rocks beset on every side.
Everywhere we turn, we're missing you;
Queer in you, we cannot now confide.
Useless though our tears are, still we weep.
Evening shadows came and now you sleep.

Herman Ogilvie Creque, 1884 – 1949 © Valerie Sims, Creque Family Archive

Mrs. Emily Creque © Creque Family Archives

Inheriting Lamesure Estate ~ 1949

After Herman passed away, Emily inherited full title to all the properties held in his name. Their Wills left everything to each other upon the death of one of the parties.

Fritz Allan Smith managed the St. John estates for her and went to St. Thomas often to give her a report on the livestock and cultivations in person. At the time, she owned over 2,500 acres on St. John, plus the islands of Little Saint James and Mingo Cay, not including acreage on Hassel Island, St. Thomas or the British Virgin Islands.

Estate Lamesure was the largest land-holding in the US Virgin Islands under one ownership and Emily now had full control.

In three years, an outsider would be knocking on her door, interested in purchasing her lands. It would be a meeting that would change the trajectory of the island's unique history.

David and Frank Stick © Outer Banks History Center, State Archives of North Carolina

The Arrival of Frank Stick ~ 1952

Frank Stick first visited St. John in the late fall of 1952 and was intrigued by the island's potential for development.

According to an article in the *Saturday Evening Post,* Frank was described as a *'gentle and friendly man in his sixties'* who was an *'accomplished illustrator, conservationist, and developer.'*

He worked closely with the National Park Service on real estate projects in Cape Hatteras, North Carolina.

Estate Reef Bay ~ 1953

Frank Stick's development plans for St. John and what he envisioned for the island were discovered by Bruce Schoonover while researching the island's history. Bruce was a member of the St. John Historical Society and was passionate about the island's history, helping to create videos and books for the organization. His wife, Sharon, kindly shared the following documents with me.

Frank Stick's plan entitled, *A Prospectus for the Development of Estate Lameshur,* discussed the specific parcels he was interested in and the price he paid for the acreage.

He first purchased a majority interest in *Estate Reef Bay* which adjoined *Lamesure* to the West. The property belonged to Frank R. Faulk and included 651.5 acres of beautiful coastline.

Frank obtained an option contract for seventy-six percent of the stock, which called for a payment of $25,000 in cash and the balance secured by a mortgage. With the acreage valued at $105,200, the price per acre was about $159.

A view of Lamesure Bay © Valerie Sims, Creque Family Archives

The Sale of Estate Lamesure ~ 1953

According to the report, the only other properties available on St. John were quoted on the bases of $300 per acre or up.

Many had no water frontage, and nothing approaching the development possibilities of *Lamesure Estate*.

Mr. and Mrs. A.R. Faulk, long-time friends, were said to have recommended *Lamesure Estate* to Frank. They had been living on St. John when they learned that *'local promoters were attempting to secure the estates.'*

Intrigued, they told Frank, who went to look at the properties. When he did, he thought the estates were ideal for a commercial development, subdivided and sold as small, vacation homes.

A view of Lamesure Estate © Valerie Sims, Creque Family Archives

Frank approached Emily '*immediately*' about securing an option to purchase them. Emily agreed and signed a binder contract for $1,000 on March 9, 1953.

The properties included the adjoining *Estates of Bakkero, Hope, Bordeaux, Great* and *Little Lamesure, Parforce, Cabritte Horn,* and *Misgunst.*

By way of a Warranty Deed on May 27, 1953, Emily formalized the transfer, however, the name on the deed was Frank's son, David Stick. David later indicated that he was the *'strawman'* for his father and other investors.

The Selling Price

The purchase sum was $80,000, or $56 per acre, considerably less than the purchase price for the adjoining *Reef Bay Estate*, at about $159 per acre.

Initially, the properties were thought to have 1,110 acres more or less, but after they were sold, a survey found them to be 1,433 acres. It is uncertain why Frank paid Mr. Faulk 283 percent more per acre for his property than he paid Emily for her lands, considering she owned the desirous beachfront he needed for his development.

Mr. Faulk may have had a survey and appraisal done before he sold and knew the true value of his lands. Perhaps Emily should have done the same.

The Mortgage

Frank paid a sum of $35,000 to Emily, and the balance of $45,000 was secured by a First Mortgage, with Emily as the Mortgagee. It was to be paid back as follows:

> $15,000 on or before the 27th day of May 1954
> $15,000 on or before the 27th day of May 1955
> $15,000 on or before the 27th day of May 1956
> Interest thereon to be computed from May 27, 1953,
> at the rate of 3% per annum

Expressly released from the terms and conditions of the Mortgage were about 200 acres, more or less. The exact location was to be determined by the parties, but the general location was the bathing beach and the buildings, together with a reasonable amount of land surrounding them. The prime beachfront acreage was Frank's main interest. He planned to subdivide the area into sellable building sites. If he defaulted on the loan, he would not lose this valuable portion of the property.

Reasons Why Emily Creque Sold

The circumstances under which Emily sold her properties is uncertain. A few reasons may have been that:

- Managing the livestock business from her permanent home in St. Thomas was difficult.
- The property taxes would have been a consideration.
- Family members were no longer spending time at the home.
- As a recent widow, she was uninterested in the livestock business or the bay tree cultivations.
- Seeing clearly was becoming difficult with her age, sixty-nine and her cataract diagnosis. Not only did she wear dark sunglasses outside, but inside the home as well.

Frank Stick's Perspective ~ April 1953

Interestingly, Frank prepared an in-depth analysis of Emily's lands before they closed on the property. Here are his findings, according to his prospectus.

- The Lamesure and adjoining estates had an excellent bathing beach and the landlocked harbor provided a safe anchorage, even under hurricane conditions.
- The highest mountain chain on the island was topped by old Bordeaux, with five valleys sweeping down to the Caribbean Sea, still covered by bay trees.
- The best and safest anchorage on the island was located in the easternmost finger of Lameshur Bay.

- The only white-sand bathing beach on the Southside was located in the middle finger of the bay.

- Behind both of these were comparatively flat areas, covered either with tropical underbrush or lofty palms and other trees.

Improvements to be Undertaken

The deed was modified to allow Frank to make changes and improvements on the property, to expedite the development plans he had in mind before he paid for the property in full.

Frank contacted the government to ascertain what assistance they could count on for their development.

- The US Soil Conservation Service agreed to determine the soil content and contour of the land.

- Conservation Service officials indicated they would probably construct, at no cost to the owners, and at a point mutually agreed upon, a reservoir suitable for supplying the water needs of the entire estate.

- A Government-owned corporation was planning to install two 100 KW generators to provide power in the Cruz Bay area and offered to extend this service. If the owners of *Lamesure Estate* were interested in connecting with the plant, the manager indicated arrangements could be made on a share-the-cost and share-the-work basis.

- Since all land surveys in the islands were made by official government surveyors, an official request was made for an outline survey, with a binder deposit of $350.00.

Clearing the Property

During the two years that Frank Stick and his partners owned the property, a great deal of clearing was done.

- Two cottages were restored and equipped with modern facilities
- Two large reservoirs were constructed. (by the US Soil Conservation Service)
- The main estate house, with eight rooms and three baths, had also been restored, except furnishings and fixtures.
- Roads for jeep travel were constructed.

Frank Stick's Development Plans

'Though there was every indication that the contract to purchase Estate Lameshur could be sold for a sizable profit, Stick and his partners considered the idea that there was a far greater potential profit to be derived from a careful, long-range development plan.' Their research indicated that the appeal of *Estate Lamesure* would be to three distinct types of potential purchasers:

- Wealthy persons interested in owning a vacation home in a quiet area, where they would be undisturbed and could take advantage of the beautiful scenery and ideal climate of St. John.
- Retired persons.
- Fishing enthusiasts interested in owning a vacation cottage in an area where they could be assured of a large variety of fish.

In early discussions, several friends and acquaintances asked to have sites set aside for them, sight unseen.

A Survey for Subdivision

Stick's investors endeavored to have a survey completed to determine the area best suitable for subdivision. In the meantime, they undertook to:

- Remodel the two small houses near the bathing beach
- Install a water system and electric power supply
- Repair existing roads and construct new ones
- Clear the bathing beach and construct temporary docking facilities
- Purchase horses, a jeep, a boat and plant coconut trees

The Lamesure Estate House © Valerie Sims, Creque Family Archives

Estate Lamesure & Others Transferred to Jackson Hole Preserve, Inc. ~ 1954

After extensively planning *Lamesure's* tourism development for over a year, Frank and his partners decided to transfer their ownership to Jackson Hole Preserve, Inc.

According to an article by Bruce Schoonover, the change of heart was due to several reasons. *'The first of which was Frank's age, seventy, his failing health, the effort and costs involved in achieving their objectives, and his son, David's lack of enthusiasm for the project.'*

On New Year's Day in 1955, *before two more mortgage payments became due* to Emily Creque, David Stick, his wife, Phyllis, and his partners, transferred the *Lamesure* properties to Jackson Hole Preserve, Inc. The silent partners were:

- Frank Stick and wife, Maud H. Stick,
- Morris A. Marks and wife, Veronique C. Marks
- Lorimer W. Midgett and wife, Margaret W. Midgett
- N.E. Aydlett and wife, Pantha H. Aydlett
- C.C. Aydlett and wife, Augusta W. Aydlett and
- The Kitty Hawk Land Co. Inc.

A stipulation was included in the Mortgage terms allowing the purchaser to pay back the mortgage earlier than the terms outlined.

Laurance Rockefeller Grateful to Frank Stick 1958

Frank Stick and his investors sold *Lamesure Estate* for approximately $194,736.00, according to the *Office of the Recorder of Deeds*. This figure was used to calculate the Stamp tax duty.

Interestingly, Frank Stick gifted his portion of the sale price, worth about $50,000, back to Rockefeller's organization, Jackson Hole Preserve, Inc.

Bruce Schoonover discovered this arrangement in a letter in which Rockefeller thanked Stick for his *'outstanding contributions to the Park effort.'* It was dated May 23, 1958.

According to the correspondence, Laurance Rockefeller acknowledged his sincere appreciation to Frank for his financial gift and the numerous hours he spent during this effort.

Frank had been working as a *volunteer,* accumulating all the lands earmarked for the *Virgin Islands National Park,* ever since he brought the *Hubler Report* to Rockefeller's attention.

Rockefeller was sure this achievement would be a *lasting satisfaction* for him.

Lamesure Estate and the surrounding lands were eventually transferred to the United States Department of the Interior.

On November 21, 1956, the estates became a part of the nation's twenty-ninth, National Park.

The Lamesure Estate House, 2015 © Valerie Sims

A Look Inside the Lamesure Home

In the summer of 2015, the National Park Ranger living at the *Lamesure* home invited my mother and I for a private tour of the estate house. This was our first visit and we were very excited.

Arrangements were made by Bob Malacarne, a friend of the ranger, Dave Horner. Bob knew how much this visit would mean to us since we were passionate about our family's history.

As the early morning sun brightened the skyline, we departed Cruz Bay together along the winding roads in anticipation of what we would discover at the home. I wondered if I would find any trace of our ancestors, perhaps some of their furniture or personal items long forgotten. Were the mahogany rocking chairs still there? Paintings? Hurricane lamps? Books? I could hardly wait to find out.

A peek at Lamesure Bay © Valerie Sims

Several times along the last bumpy stretch of dirt road, I thought our vehicle would stall. There were so many rocks on the road, I thought surely a flat tire was inevitable. Was this property even accessible? It seemed unlikely that anyone would ever leave for groceries and supplies once they arrived. Surely, they must be air-dropped in!

As we approached the beach, we stood in awe at its beauty. The seabirds chirped and flew overhead as the pelicans dove only feet away from the beach. Their incredible accuracy always amazed me, especially in such shallow water.

It was a crystal-clear day as we toured through the ruins, posing and taking a few photographs to remember our visit. The historic structures, with their open window spaces to the sea, formed pretty picturesque frames of the blue ocean beyond.

I tried to locate the ruins of the bay oil distillery. Could it be in one of these stone foundations? They seemed more appropriate as living quarters, rather than a distillery house or workroom.

We continued up the treacherous, rocky road in four-wheel drive, a great deterrent to any visitors or trespassers. After a few more hairpin turns, we came upon the brow of the hill where a solid concrete structure stood.

Flanking the house was the most beautiful Flamboyant tree in full bloom! The limbs seemed to embrace the home, curling around the windows and eaves to form an umbrella of vibrant, orange colors. What a welcoming sight!

We approached the front door and knocked, eagerly awaiting a response. I thought about Herman and Emily and how wonderful it would have been to know them personally. I'd spent a lifetime researching their lives but never had the opportunity to meet them. They both passed before I was born. Ranger Dave opened the door with a smile, and as we walked in, we thanked him profusely for our special opportunity.

The Lamesure home where the pergola once stood. © Valerie Sims

He invited us to sit down on the sofa and as we did, we looked around in amazement, allowing ourselves to be transported back in time. If only the thick, concrete walls could talk and tell us what they had witnessed.

We asked Ranger Dave about his experiences living in such a remote location far away from town. He didn't seem to mind and preferred the quiet sounds of his surroundings.

In anticipation of our visit, he shared a few documents about the property's history that he had on the coffee table.

The Home's Builder ~ 1832

The original construction of the home was thought to be around 1832, when a Danish Councilor, Ingjald C. J. Mourier, was the highest bidder.

He first arrived in St. Thomas in 1825 when his brother was the Commander at the Fort and was persuaded to stay.

According to David W. Knight Sr.'s research, Mourier carried the news of emancipation, visiting the *Estates of Adrian and Rustenburg*. They were *'the first to learn of their newly won freedom.'*

Touring the Home

Ranger Dave proceeded to show us around beginning with the front balcony facing the sea. This was the room once furnished with rocking chairs and small tables. I had high hopes of seeing some of the furniture, but sadly, they were gone.

As I looked around, the room seemed so much smaller than I imagined. I had pictured a huge, spacious verandah in my mind, a scenic place where everyone kept a keen lookout for Herman's boat when it returned from the day's journey.

The panorama was beautiful, as I imagined sailing sloops tacking past the harbor's entrance.

Herman and Emily were long gone, but I kept looking for clues that something of theirs might still be there. I wanted desperately to connect with them. When I spotted a small detail on the wooden ceiling that I had seen in photographs, it made me smile.

Above where a small dining table once stood, was a round metal hook. It looked like it had been painted over many times throughout the years. From this hook, a kerosene lamp once hung long ago, illuminating and casting shadows over the table and its occupants.

Tiny as the clue was, it was the affirmation I was looking for that this was their home. I wasn't dreaming. I was standing in a place where the family had previously lived and loved.

Could it be that seated under this very hook was where Captain Romer shared tantalizing details of his solo journey across the Atlantic? This must have been the spot where they had bonded over Tardy's home-cooked meals and laughter, becoming better acquainted.

An Apparition in the Doorway

Off the verandah was a narrow doorway where Emily's eldest daughter, Olga, had once stood for a photograph.

Emily, Henry and Olga at Lamesure Estate, St. John © Creque Family Archives

Ranger Dave shared an interesting story about this very entrance. It led to a basement area where the washing machine and storage items were kept.

He told us that an overnight visitor in the home once saw an apparition of a female figure in this same doorway! Naturally, he was quite concerned and wary about staying. As scary as this experience might have been, it didn't seem surprising to me.

Almost every home our ancestors lived in had paranormal activity at one time or another.

Looking for a Connection

Perusing through the rest of the rooms, exploring and imagining what life was like for the family, was exciting for my mother and me. Even Bob was enjoying the tour!

As I peeked around each corner, I secretly hoped I would find something more linking us to our loved ones. I am forever grateful to Ranger Dave and Bob for giving us the opportunity of reconnecting with a part of our family's past. *Lamesure Estate* will always be a special place for us.

Finding a Clue

As I was preparing this manuscript and perusing photographs taken during our visit, I spotted two objects I'm certain once belonged to Herman and Emily!

They were the ornate, concrete planters that flanked the doorway entrance facing the sea. I'm surprised I hadn't recognized them earlier! Almost every home belonging to various family members had these identical planters outside. We had several of them outside of our own home growing up.

Around the upper border were uniquely raised patterns of multiple scrolls that reminded me of the petroglyphs found at Reef Bay. These planters were popular in the 1920s and the family had more than 300 of them around their various homes on St. Thomas, Hassel Island, and St. John. They were a perfect pot for flowers and greenery and framed the background of many of the family's photographs. Two of them were perched on the upstairs balcony at the Francis Bay home when the family stayed there.

Posing by the Planter Pots

It's wonderful to know that a small contribution from the Creque family's occupation now lives on at the *Lamesure Estate* house.

Diane Mawson, my mother's sister poses by the concrete planters © Creque Family Archives

Chapter 5

Purchasing Mary's Point ~ 1927

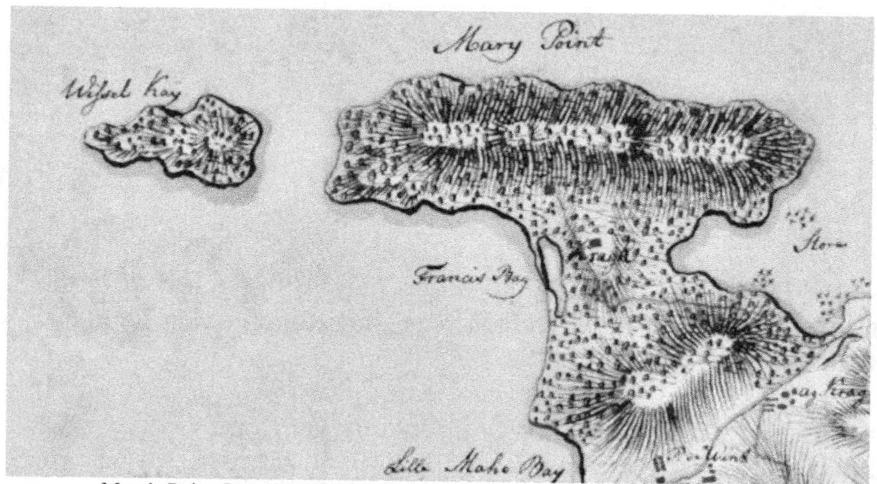

Mary's Point, Peter Lotharius Oxholm Map, 1780 © The Royal Library of Denmark

One of the most recognizable estates on St. John is the beautiful peninsula known as *Mary's Point.* From the sea where this promontory stands, one can marvel at the green, grassy hillsides, a true landmark for passing sailors.

Small boats often used the narrow cut between *Whistling Cay* and *Mary's Point* because the water was much smoother and calmer. I certainly did whenever I traveled between Tortola and Cruz Bay on my boat. Hugging this coastline on the way to Cruz Bay or returning home to the British Virgins made navigation easier for me.

To appreciate the history of the estate, here is a brief overview, beginning with the development plans Carl Francis and others envisioned for their fertile estate before Herman's purchase in 1927.

Landowners of Mary's Point Estate

- George and Lucy Francis, 1877 – 1895
- Carl and George Francis, 1895 – 1907
- Luther Stakemann, 1907 – 1927
- Herman O. Creque and Family, 1927 – 1954
- Jackson Hole Preserve, Inc 1954 – 1956
- Virgin Islands National Park, 1956 – Today

Carl E. Francis, 1867 ~ 1936

In June 1894, *Mary's Point Estate* was put up for auction after the passing of the owner and widow, Mrs. Lucy Francis, on February 10, 1894.

On January 22, 1895, two of her children, Carl and George Fritz Allen Francis, became the new proprietors of 250 acres of pasture lands and dense woodlands. They paid 350 West Indian dollars.

Carl Emmanuel Francis was a true native of St. John, admired and revered by many for his untiring efforts to help those less fortunate.

He moved to Santo Domingo in 1890 for work and was *'employed in a responsible post on one of the best estates on the island.'* After twelve years working in the Dominican Republic, he returned home on July 22, 1902, aboard the sloop, *Fame*. The newspaper editor was very happy, '*Carl belongs to St. John, and is bound home,'* he wrote.

Business there, Carl said, was in *'a visibly declining state, owing principally to the unremunerative price of sugar. Wages were cut down to the lowest level and living expenses remained high.'*

Carl Francis © The Royal Library of Denmark

The Plantain Farm ~ 1902

Carl returned to St. John with grand ideas for a new enterprise on his estates of *Annaberg* and *Mary's Point.* He intended to establish a plantain farm on an extensive scale and imported 2,000 plantain slips, transporting them with him on the *Fame,* from the Dominican Republic.

He also brought several laborers who had practical knowledge in cultivating this valuable food.

His fine estates had fertile land and he believed in the profitability of this venture. The newspaper editors thought it was, *'a very bright idea'* too. In time, they hoped to *'hear of its complete success and see St. John plantains take the place of foreign importations sold in the local markets and St. Croix.'*

By 1903, Carl had '*large tracts of land under fine cultivation,'* including fifty-one of his plantain slips which were bearing fruit. He also cultivated large plots with black-eyed peas, some of which were shipped in barrels for export.

He began growing sweet potatoes too. Carl was hard at work all the time! His latest effort was the plantain of the so-called Donkey banana, the kind most suitable for use by the Danish West Indian Fruit Company. The newspaper editors continually supported his efforts. *'We are glad to hear that Mr. Francis is getting on successfully.'*

The Donkey Banana

The *Donkey* banana or *Burro* banana is a short, chunky banana, compared to the common banana we know of today. Its stubby stature is reminiscent of a donkey's ear. Its peel is a rich, vivid, dark green that turns deep yellow with characteristic black spots when ripe.

When young, it was tart and tangy with creamy-sweet lemon undertones. They were versatile and people used to enjoy them fresh or green, like a plantain. This fruit was a perfect choice for cultivation due to its superior, hardy nature and wind-resistant foliage.

The Agricultural Exhibition ~ 1903

'The hoe and the spade, the shovel and rake, when handled aright, will a nobleman make.'

As the plantain crop was maturing, Carl learned of an interesting exhibition being organized in St. Thomas. It was being promoted as *The Second Agricultural and Industrial Society Exhibition.*

The object of the exhibition was to bring together *'products of the soil'*, as well as local handicrafts, to give the Royal Commissioners visiting from the Mother Country an idea of the agricultural possibilities in the islands.

When the exhibition opened in Coconut Park, Carl and various estate owners and laborers entered with their homegrown produce.

St. John Made a Big Showing

'Considering the dry weather and short notice, the country folks did very well, and it was pleasing to see what a large and varied display St. John made.'

There were huge displays, both in the park and in the Apollo Theatre. *'The scene was like a grand garden party and at night, the illuminations transformed it into a sort of fairyland.'*

The Livestock Exhibition

Both Henry O. Creque and Herbert E. Lockhart closed their St. Thomas stores to participate in the exhibition, bringing the best examples of their breeding cattle for display.

Additional animals were tethered to the pilings around the park, including fine specimens of bulls, cows, horses, ponies, mules, donkeys, hogs and a very handsome and well-cared-for group of Angora rabbits, belonging to Emil Eloi. The animals all together numbered about fifty-eight.

A view of Coconut Park, St. Thomas, Danish West Indies © A.H. Riise Postcard

The Beautifully Decorated Park

The park was beautifully adorned with hundreds of colored lanterns suspended from wires, strung high from tree to tree. The fairy-like appearance combined with the brilliance of the lights produced the most delightful, panoramic effect.

The exhibition lasted two days and nights with huge crowds that presented a scene of 'much gaiety and picturesqueness.'

All enjoyed 'the fine music, refreshments and snowballs that wiled the pleasant hours away.'

The Prize Winners

Winning first prize for the largest exhibit was Henry D. McDonald of *Hawksnest Estate*. He received $8.00 for his *'special industry, energy, and perseverance in the work of cultivation.'*

Basket weavers on St. John © A Lightbourn Postcard

Carl Francis took the second prize for his display of plantains, freshly churned butter, honey, and wax and received $3.00. A fine display of oranges and cane syrup won $3.00 for John E. Lindqvist of *America Hill*, near Cinnamon Bay.

St. John was well represented among the eighty-five exhibitors. Displayed were corn, bananas, potatoes, yams, cassava, pineapples, soursops, oranges, lemons, and limes.

Manufactured items included baskets, table mats, doormats and walking sticks made by hand from different local woods. One special entry was a mongoose, *'the pest of St. John.'*

Many thanks went to Lawyer Jorgensen who was credited with coming up with the idea for the exhibition. It proved to be a resounding success!

Honorable Mentions

The following participants received honorable mentions for their contributions from St. John.
Miss Zelma Roberts – Basketwork, Miss Izza Penn – Spanish work, Miss Lottie Clen – Crochet and Agave work, Ernest Sewer – Basketwork, Edith Francis – Basketwork, William H. Marsh – Bay oil, Miss Hennessy – Coconut oil, and B. White – Cassavas

A Miniature Model ~ 1903

Franklin George, a thirteen-year-old boy, built a beautiful model of the sailing yacht, *Sea Fox,* for the exhibition. The judges were very impressed with the miniature sailboat and awarded Franklin $2.00.

Anson Phelps Stokes, a notable yachtsman, had been on a cruise through the West Indies, sailing from New York to Trinidad, when he anchored at Francis Bay.

He was an enthusiastic admirer of the '*wonderful beauty and coral sand beaches'* of the islands. Young Franklin must have been impressed when he saw the yacht, using its design for his inspiration.

A Display of Unity

Amid beautiful weather and boundless enthusiasm, the committee thanked Reverend, Edward B. Foster of the Dutch Reformed Church for his untiring efforts to collect all the exhibits and promote the show.

It was an incredible display of unity by the industrious inhabitants on this little island. It would not be the last time the community came together to proudly present the fruits of their harvest.

The Francis Family Sells Mary's Point Estate

The families of Luther Stakemann and Carl Francis at Mary's Point © Marian Czukoski

By 1906, Carl wished to have his co-ownership in *Mary's Point* dissolved and put the estate up for auction. Luther Stakemann of St. Thomas, a very close friend of Carl's, was the highest bidder, paying $1,500 for the property in 1907.

Luther Emanuel Stakemann, 1870 ~ 1927

Luther Stakemann was a Senior Clerk, appointed in charge of the firm of *J.H. Fechtenburg* on Main Street in St. Thomas. He began working for the company as a teenager.

J.H. Fechtenburg sold a variety of foodstuffs like flour, margarine, Ferris hams, and bacon, as well as delicacies like Danish Dried Cherries, chocolates and Marie biscuits.

According to the *St. Thomas Mail Notes*, "*by a dint of hard work and an unequalled display of business ability, Luther rapidly climbed the rungs of the ladder of success to a partnership in the firm.*"

Luther's family was well established in the islands, with a long and distinctive history. A distant relative, born in 1805 in St. Thomas, was Johan August Stakemann. He held the honor of *Knight of Dannebrog* and was Vice-Governor of the islands in the 1870s. Like his ancestor, Luther was very active in the community and popular on all three islands.

He was a member of the Colonial Council, the Carnival Committee, the St. Thomas Boating Club and first tenor in the Singing Club, performing in several parish halls in St. Thomas. The sweet sounds of his high voice very likely reverberated through the pastures and hilltops during his summer stays at Mary's Point.

In his spare time, he was Treasurer of the St. Thomas Cricket Association and was an accomplished cricket player himself, admired for his "*moving spirit in all matters of local cricket.*"

In 1906, he was appointed a member of the St. Thomas Harbor Board and a few years later, became active in politics.

Luther was kind and helpful to many of his fellow citizens. In 1922, he offered twenty acres of his *Mary's Point Estate* for free to natives of St. John and St. Thomas who wished to cultivate the land to help support their families.

Five years later, when he passed away on May 5, 1927, many were heartbroken after learning of his sudden demise. According to his obituary in the *St. Thomas Mail Notes*, he was remembered as a man who *"loved his country and did his best."*

Estella Stakemann © Marian Czukoski

Estella Stakemann

Shortly after Luther's death, his *Mary's Point Estate* was probated in favor of his widow, Estella and appraised at a value of $3,750. Wishing to sell the property she was awarded, Estella thought of Herman and his possible interest since both families had known each other for a very long time. Both Luther and Herman loved cricket and played on *The St. Thomas New CC team* together. Herman was nineteen years old and Luther, thirty-three, and a member of the management committee.

A view over Francis Bay, St. John, US Virgin Islands © Creque Family Archives

Herman Creque Purchases the Property ~ 1927

Intrigued by the beauty of Estella's lands and the potential to expand his livestock business even further, on June 27, 1927, the two agreed on a purchase price of $6,500. It was a significant sum above its court-appraised value.

The 250-acre estate included all the livestock; however, specifically excluded was all the furniture and other personal household effects from the Francis Bay home.

Historically, almost 200 years had passed since the *Slave Insurrection of 1733*, when many of the captives met their deaths over the rocky promontory.

Chapter 6

Acquiring Annaberg Estate ~ 1932

Annaberg Estate © Creque Family Archives

You may recall from Chapter Two that Carl Francis was the highest bidder for *Annaberg Estate* when Eugène's properties were probated in 1899. Carl divided it, selling:

- 50 acres (20%) to Herbert E. Lockhart for $625 in 1925, and
- 197 acres (80%) to Herman, Eugène's grandson for $2,250 in 1932.

Herbert E. Lockhart, Sr. ~ 1927

Herbert E. Lockhart, '*a tall figure*', was a prominent businessman and influential merchant in St. Thomas and owned many estates on St. John.

Both Honorable Lockhart and Honorable Creque were members of the Colonial Council and were well acquainted with each other. By 1940, they also shared duties in the Cricket Association, with Lockhart as President and Creque as Vice-President.

Herman O. Creque ~ 1935

Herbert knew his neighbor was interested in expanding his grazing lands and when he wanted to sell the fifty acres he'd purchased from Carl, he offered him the first option.

Appreciating the gesture, Herman agreed and paid $900, in March 1935. This gave Herman and Emily complete ownership of the entire *Annaberg Estate*, which comprised 247 acres.

With *Mary's Point* included, the family owned approximately 500 acres of the loveliest land on the northwest side of St. John. Francis Bay became their children's favorite spot and was the most beautiful bathing beach one could desire, merely a stone's throw from their home. Later, it became their grandchildren's favorite as well.

Emily and Herman Creque © Valerie Sims, Creque Family Archives

The home, years after it was transferred to the V.I. National Park © The Library of Congress

The Francis Bay Home

The family's home was quaint and charming, with all the island character one expected from a remote cottage built many years prior. It was located on the right side of a narrow walking trail, which curved around the pond to the sparkling bay.

Unlike buildings from the early twentieth century, the kitchen was attached to the structure. This was Tardy's domain. As mentioned earlier in this book, she was an incredible cook and prepared the most delicious meals there.

Inside the House

At one time, there were two stories with the top floor made of wooden panels in a hexagonal shape. This was where the children's bedroom was located, with access by way of a staircase set behind the house. This large room had a stunning view of the sea and was equipped with two large beds. Downstairs was the master bedroom and two small rooms with one bathroom for the entire home.

Near the cistern was a wooden structure where Alphonse Harley and Morris Nicholson stayed when overnighting. Harley was a foreman at the Creque Railway, and Morris helped to keep the yard and property pruned.

Much of the home has deteriorated over the years, but I remember being able to look inside before it started to collapse.

The living and dining rooms on the main floor were partitioned with three-quarter high walls and the space above was covered with white lattice, allowing air to circulate throughout the house. This design kept it cool during the hot summer months. The roof has since caved in, but the verandah, with its Spanish, mosaic tile, is still in good condition.

Interestingly, this identical tile can be found in the *St. Anne's Catholic Church* in Frenchtown, St. Thomas, built in 1921. The pattern was also used in the family's home in St. Thomas.

The covered porch was where everyone gathered after a long day in the sun, with a conveniently grown lime tree tucked in the corner behind the veranda. It produced the juiciest limes for their special, home-made cocktails. Limeade, mixed with Virgin Islands' rum, was their favorite refreshment.

Inside the Francis Bay Home © Valerie Sims

Home Improvements ~ 1942

This home meant the world to the family and was at the heart of all their wonderful memories. When it needed attention, Herman organized with the workmen to replace several doors and windows.

Jotted on the diary's sideline were the dimensions for a new pantry door (69 x 35 ¾), a western bathroom window (38 x 30) and a southern bathroom window, (38 x 24). John Prince, Wally Jackson, and Lucien Johannes were hired for the job.

Herman was meticulous about these log entries. He used sixteen gallons of white paint on the house, costing him $40.00, 4 paintbrushes, $1.50/each, 1 wire brush, 25 cents, 3 pounds of galvanized, shingle nails, 30 cents/pound and 2 padlocks valued at 20 cents.

The Pattern on the Patio Tiles

Patio tiles at the Francis Bay home © Valerie Sims

Frank Creque at Francis Bay © Creque Family Archives

Frank D. Creque

During the early 1950s, Herman's youngest son, Frank lived at the home, overseeing the livestock and the lands. After he moved away, the property was made available as a furnished cottage for rent with the use of a cabin cruiser.

The advertisement read, *'Mary's Point Estate, available accommodations for two to six people. Furnished with an outboard, canoe, horses, and donkeys.'*

Fun times await; *lobstering, rock fishing, trolling, and conch diving* on a private beach. *'See Frank Creque at Hibiscus Alley, Beretta Center, St. Thomas, US Virgin Islands.'*

The livestock © Creque Family Archives

The Blue Diary

Herman kept a detailed journal of his livestock venture in a small, blue diary that he carried everywhere. He noted the quantities and weights of the animals he owned, as well as his purchases and sales of them. The sale of nine goats, for instance, generated $16. After $2.50 for catching them and another $2 for shipping them was deducted, it left a small profit, which he noted on April 9, 1935.

Other entries in the 1930s included:

- The sale of a bull to Mr. L.C. Matta of Lovango Cay for $18, and later that year, ten cows from Mary's Point for $190.
- The sale of four donkeys for $4.75 each to a purchaser in Jost van Dyke.
- The purchase of a bull from Charles Smith for $25 as well as two additional bulls, weighing 425 pounds and 390 pounds respectively, for $40.00 each.

New Cattle Pricing by the Pound ~ 1930s

The diary also recorded a new pricing schedule for the sale of livestock that raised the prices slightly. For all animals up to 540 pounds, 500 pounds would be considered as calves and priced at twelve cents per pound, and the difference would be treated as cows, at eleven cents per pound. This meant an animal weighing 540 pounds would have realized a price of $64.40, an increase of about ten dollars. It was a full-time job keeping track of all the accounting for this business, but this was a task Herman enjoyed.

Expanding the Cattle Business, 1933 – 1948

Not only did Herman keep a hand-written diary of his activities at *Lamesure Estate*, but he also jotted down his activities at *Mary's Point* from the 1930s to the 1940s.

Since the area was known for the *'best and most inexhaustible water supply'* on the island, he had the overgrown brush surrounding the bay cleared to build animal enclosures.

He transferred some of the livestock from *Lamesure* to increase the breeding supply and expand his business.

In 1934, he hired Fritz Jackson, Daniel Jackson, Lucien Johannes, Wally Jackson and Charles Bastian to clear the land. Together, they installed 5,000 feet of wire fencing, creating three enclosures.

They started from the eastern gate surrounding Francis Bay and extended to *Mary's Point*. It was a big job with labor expenses totaling $110. Forty rolls of wire mesh were used, adding $100 in materials. These three enclosures secured over 130 animals.

Raising Beef Cattle

Raising cattle was advantageous, given that it provided both food for the family and laborers, as well as profits for the company. A single animal yielded from 300 to 550 pounds of meat. They required an enormous amount of fresh clean water, as well as lush pasture and shade during the hottest part of the day. A nursing cow, for instance, could drink up to twenty gallons of water a day, depending on her size.

Cattle rearing was a demanding business and involved an in-depth knowledge of breeding techniques. Herman knew the business well and acquainted himself with all the common cattle ailments. Diseases such as parasites and various infections could make the difference to the success of this venture.

The livestock at Lamesure Estate © Creque Family Archives

Introducing A New Breed of Cattle

During the early 1900s, a new breed of livestock was developed on the island of St. Croix. Cows from Senegal, Africa were crossbred with Red Poll bulls from England. Crossbreeding produced, in just one or two generations, what it would take many generations to achieve in purebred animals. This was a useful tool since no single breed had all the best traits needed for beef production in the islands.

Senepol Cattle

The result was a cattle breed called, *Senepol*. They were medium-sized animals noted for heat and parasite resistance, perfect for the island's climate. They had a docile nature, good meat, and high milk yield.

The average calf at *Mary's Point* weighed between 300 and 400 pounds, with larger adult animals reaching upwards of 1,000 pounds.

While the specific type of cattle Herman was raising is uncertain, his livestock inventory may have included a quantity of this new island breed. Mr. Lockhart, who owned *Estate Hermitage*, was grazing a quantity of Senepol bulls on his property.

The Cost of Supplies

Everything Herman purchased, he marked with written notations. Tools, like a shovel, for instance, he recorded the price, $1.20, a rake $1.00, machete $1.20, a can of paint $2.50 and a bag of cement for 80 cents.

His journal proved invaluable for an insider's look at the livestock business that we never would have known.

The Animal Inventory at Mary's Point

The inventory for the estate in August of 1934 consisted of:
51 Cows • 27 Bulls • 26 Heifers • 21 Heifer Calves and 7 Bull Calves for a total of 132 animals.

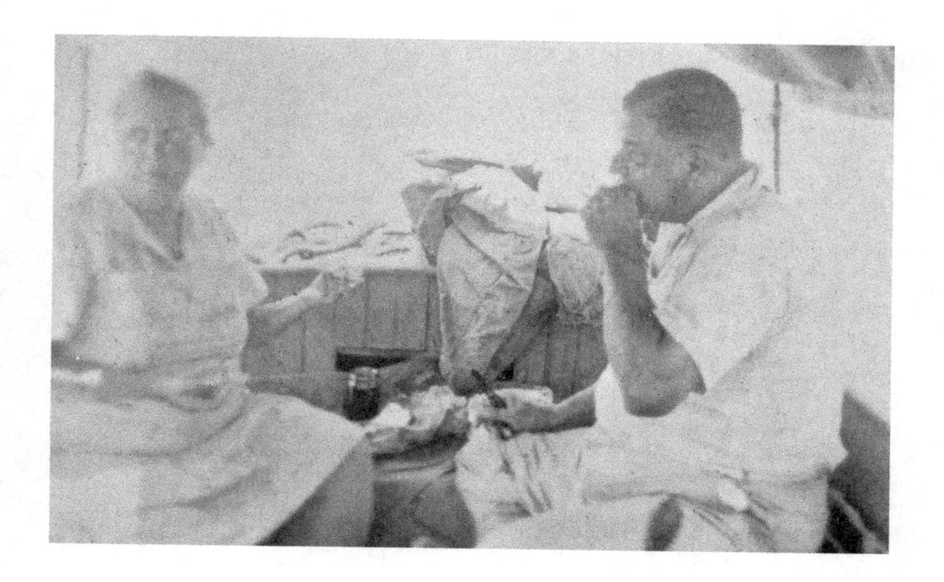

Fishing Together for Fun ~ 1930s

When not working or hunting, Herman enjoyed spending time with his wife. They were fond of each other and shared many similar hobbies. Best friends since they first met in their early twenties, they shared a passion for boating and fishing, which included many excursions to various out-islands.

Interestingly, Emily always wore a dress and ankle boots wherever she went, even out on the boat. She never wore pants and saved her best shoes for Sunday mass.

Although Madam was the *Lady of the House*, she was quite adventurous. She enjoyed fishing trips and was adept at baiting her hook and untangling monofilament line when the need arose.

Here she is, anchored over a familiar reef as the two readied their tackle for a day of bottom-fishing together. Hand-lining was one of the oldest and simplest forms of fishing and brought lots of enjoyment and excitement for them, especially when a fish took the bait and bolted.

M/V St. John © Creque Family Archives

The St. John Motor Launch ~ 1930s

Herman spent a lot of time on the sea, traveling between the islands for business and pleasure.

On many occasions, when he was motoring to St. John from Redhook, he passed the administrator's boat as it was heading back to port. It was a picket boat called, the *m/v St. John*. He knew the captain from the days when the vessel was hauled at the railway. When he saw him, he often brought the *Chips* within shouting distance for a casual greeting on the sea.

Picket boats were a small type of military craft used for harbor patrol and close shoreline work.

In 1948, a vessel similar to the one pictured was given to the municipality by the US Coast Guard and assigned to the St. John administrator for official travel. William Blackwood was appointed the captain and engineer of the new boat, with Cruz Bay as its home port.

These types of wooden crafts were self-bailing, but not self-righting, so the captain had to be careful in rough seas. It carried two crew and a maximum of ten passengers, which were accommodated when the vessel was not needed for official use.

This image may be that of Margaret Casey Gates at Caneel Bay © Creque Family Archives

American Artists Arrive ~ 1936

Both Herman and his eldest son, Henry took many photographs of their adventures on St. John and their albums overflowed with fascinating pictures of interesting people.

Not every photograph was labeled, which made identifying them very difficult. This photograph, taken at Caneel Bay, may be that of Margaret Gates, a visiting artist from Washington DC.

Robert Franklin Gates and his wife Margaret were both members of a special group working under the *Works Progress Administration*, spearheaded by President Franklin D. Roosevelt.

They arrived with the intention of creating watercolors that would capture the island's scenic beauty to give the American public an idea of what the islands were like. They hoped to make them more attractive to tourists to help boost the economy.

Robert F. Gates and Margaret C. Gates

Robert won many awards for his artworks, which were exhibited around the world in museums, federal buildings, and private collections.

Grazing donkeys at Caneel Bay © Margaret Casey Gates

While he painted several pretty scenes of St. Thomas during their stay, Margaret made several sketches and vivid watercolors of picturesque spots on St. John. In her notebook was an unfinished watercolor of two donkeys she encountered at Caneel Bay.

While I can't say definitively that the photograph on the previous page is one of Mrs. Gates, there is a strong similarity between the two beach scenes. Today, her watercolors form part of an interesting collection held at the Archives of American Art in Washington DC.

A Lasting Legacy ~ 1949

Over the years, Herman built a thriving business selling livestock by the pound. His journal was filled with transactions regarding the sales and purchases of animals.

It's very evident he loved what he was doing on St. John. He juggled all his businesses, hiring the best overseers to keep them going. When he wasn't there himself, he had one of his trusted caretakers make sure everything ran smoothly.

He traveled constantly back and forth between the US and British Virgins, hauling supplies, transporting laborers and taking his family out for special excursions.

Herman's favorite boat was the *Condor*, although he used the *Chips* more frequently for fishing and transportation.

The *m/v Condor* at Caneel Bay © Creque Family Archives

A Final Farewell

According to Herman's grandson, Henry Owen Creque, IV, when Herman passed away, the *Condor* was painted black in mourning for him and never used again. His son, Henry built a boathouse for it at the railway and there it sat for years until the roof collapsed and the boat sank. This gesture by Henry was a final farewell to his father.

Chapter 7

Fun Times at Francis Bay ~ 1927

The siblings with a friend at Francis Bay in 1927 © Creque Family Archives

Herman and Emily's children had the most amazing times at the Francis Bay home. It was simply magical for them.

Olga, Val, Henry, Frank, and Margie didn't see the property as a livelihood, the way their father did. It was their playground, their escape.

They spent their summers as young teens chasing each other and splashing around in the crystal-clear sea. Their laughter and giggles could be heard at the house, which was set back quite a distance from the beach. In those days, all the trees and brush were kept low so that the home had a clear view of the ocean.

Those were happy, carefree days when winning a race to the farthest end of the beach was the kids' only concern. As they bolted along the beautiful bay, they passed schools of minnows and trumpet fish that lurked in the shallows. With every splash from their heels, the slender, iridescent fish darted back towards safety in the deep.

The Beautiful Bay

A few yards in the shimmery distance, curious turtles popped their heads up for air and a quick, cautionary glance at the horizon, seemingly aware of what the children were doing.

Sometimes graceful stingrays made their way to shore, cruising the shallows to feed on smaller snails and crabs. Francis Bay was always teaming with marine life!

Mary's Creek © Creque Family Archives

Friends at Francis Bay

Val invited her girlfriends from St. Thomas to stay with them and they loved to chitchat, spending their days gossiping and sharing trivialities.

In the late afternoons, they rode along *Mary's Creek* together on the backs of their slow-moving mules. The stubborn animals always followed the contour of the bay, never going in the desired direction. It didn't matter though; the camaraderie the friends shared was what was most important to them.

Valerie Creque and a friend at the beach, 1930s © Creque Family Archives

Emily Creque on the Redhook Pier, St. Thomas © Valerie Sims, Creque Family Archives

A Fine Fisherwoman

Fishing was fun and Val was an excellent fisherwoman, often using soldier crab tails for bait. Nothing was wasted and the remnants were crushed to make chum.

Val was very adventurous and wasn't fussy about baiting her hook or taking her catches off the line when she caught a fish. The Redhook pier was one of her favorite fishing spots. She loved to toss her line over in the hopes of pulling up something surprising.

One day, she got quite a scare when she discovered that a Conger eel had coiled around her hook. Bravely, she removed it with a stick and casually threw it back in the water. In those bygone days, the area was known as *Shark Wharf* and rightly so, as sharks were often caught and skinned there, part of a small farming industry.

Val wasn't afraid of the sharks; she caught a few. What she didn't like were the swarms of mosquitoes that infested the area. To keep them from biting her, she lit a few cigarettes, using them as mosquito coils, hoping it would help.

Like her brother Henry, she was an entertaining conversationalist and a lot of fun to be around. Witty and smart, she could match anyone in an argument with a quick retort, especially her family.

The Creque siblings and spouses at the Francis Bay home © Creque Family Archives

Vacations on the Verandah ~ 1930s

When adults, the siblings continued to vacation together with their spouses, laughing, reminiscing, and having a silly time together on the verandah. It was a place for them to unwind as they sat along the concrete balustrade, hip to hip, chatting late into the evenings.

So many special memories were made there. Francis Bay was unique, unlike Hassel Island where they'd lived during some of their formative years.

On Hassel, when the steam boiler started churning at daybreak and the chains began rattling, it was noisy and sometimes unbearable. Once the men began their daily work, the smell of tar being applied to the hulls permeated the home and they were glad they'd taken the small cobble over to school. The railway was not the ideal playground for young children.

Val, two friends, Olga, and Arnold van Beverhoudt © Creque Family Archives

The nearby shoreline where they went to escape after school was rocky and uninviting, very unlike Francis Bay where the softest sand beckoned them to sit and relax for hours.

Lamesure was fun during the time they spent there, but it was very quiet and isolated. From the bay, there was nothing to see on the horizon and they felt very alone.

Francis Bay was perfect! Val walked the beach 1,000 times, admiring the alluring shades of blue that softly rippled on the shore. She wrote many of her poems after those long strolls, absorbing the serenity and natural beauty that surrounded her.

When she became a mother in the mid-1930s, her young girls spent their summers at Francis Bay too. Those memories of running free, playing and laughing made Francis Bay synonymous with love. Love for the outdoors, love for their family, for fun, laughter and for life itself. No place in the world compared to the wonderful memories of innocent, playful times spent at Francis Bay.

As the sisters and girlfriends chatted and swapped stories, their brothers spent their time fishing and hunting with friends.

Margie Creque at Francis Bay, St. John © Creque Family Archives

Give Me a Place

Poems from A Small Island

Give me a place wherever it be
Where I can see the rolling sea.

Give me a place where I can lie
And see the stars shine in the sky.

Give me a place where I can rest
And see a hill's green, grassy crest.

Give me a place where I can hear
The songbird's song so sweet and clear.

Give me a place where I can lie
And see the fleecy clouds go by.

Give me a place where lots of trees
Are always whispering in the breeze.

Give me this place to be my own
And I will always call it home.

If all these things I did possess,
My cup would brim with happiness.

Frank Creque holding a hardnose he caught at Mary's Creek © Creque Family Archives

Frank Creque and Dante de Lagarde © Creque Family Archives

Fishing and Hunting

The men in the family loved the outdoors and cherished their time with each other, fishing and hunting.

When they returned to the house after a day on the sea or foraging through the brush, they divided their catches with the workers' families who always appreciated a fresh meal.

The boys caught everything from mountain doves, pigeons, and wild goats, to kingfish, crabs, and conch! Herman's sons, Henry and Frank were expert marksmen and had been taught how to handle a rifle and a fishing rod when they were young boys.

Hunting on Hassel Island ~ 1931

Despite their abilities as avid sportsmen, there was a terrible accident that occurred when the boys were teenagers. When Henry was nineteen, he was careless with his aim and almost seriously hurt someone.

He was hunting wild birds on Hassel Island one day when one of his bullets strayed across the harbor and hit a bystander. Everyone was shocked; Henry's stray bullet had grazed the neck of the British Consul while he stood by his window some 300 feet away!

It was an unbelievably close call. Thankfully, *'the bullet, being small, did not make a serious wound.'*

The St. Thomas Rifle Club ~ 1935

With a little more experience and maturity, Henry formed the *St. Thomas Rifle Club* so he could practice with cousins and family friends as often as possible.

Dante de Lagarde, Eugène's grandson, was a cousin who accompanied the brothers on hunting trips. He loved the sport too.

Their group used to practice at their west-end shooting range in St. Thomas, which they nicknamed *Camp Brewers.* They enjoyed their target competitions against the St. Croix Rifle Club, the USMC team, and the USCG Marion team when the ship was in port.

The boys could stand for hours under the blistering sun, practicing and hitting bulls-eye targets, twenty-five, and fifty yards away.

At different times, the winning title went back and forth among the participating teams, but everyone enjoyed those exciting displays of true sportsmanship.

The Shooting Accident ~ 1935

Despite their growing expertise, yet another accident happened while hunting. This one almost cost the life of one of their closest friends.

Henry Creque and Dante de Lagarde © Creque Family Archives

One of the club members missed their target and accidentally wounded Dante, sending scatter shots into his legs and chest. When Dante finally recovered and was out of harm's way, the story became a joke the boys shared.

There was never a dull moment when they reminisced about their adventures—and they certainly had plenty of them!

White-Tailed Deer

White-tailed deer were one of the most graceful and elegant animals to hunt.

Whenever they sensed danger nearby, they raised their large, distinctive tails to warn predators to stay away.

Desmond Fabio, President of the Rifle Club, brought in the first deer of the 1935 season after stalking it for hours. It weighed about eighty pounds, enough to feed his family with extra meat to share.

No one is certain exactly when the White-Tail first arrived in the islands.

As early as the 1840s, a visitor, James Smith, noted their presence in the mountainous parts of St. Croix.

Hunting for Zenaida Doves

Henry enjoyed hunting for Zenaida doves too since they were easy to spot and delicious to eat. Their plumage was largely reddish to brownish and their sounds were very distinctive.

They sang with a gentle, mournful-sounding cooing, described as 'coo-ooo, coo, coo, coo' or 'hoo-ooo, ooo ooo, ooo.'

He could hear them before he spotted them in the thickets and shrubby areas when they nested in the low branches of the trees. They were quite plentiful around *Mary's Point.*

To catch them, he awoke early and headed out at dawn. Sometimes, he waited till dusk when he knew the birds would be active. Either way, he was undetected in the camouflaged clothing that he always wore.

His brother and friends tagged along too, which made locating the fallen birds easier because it was difficult to find them by himself once they fell into the overgrown brush. Besides, chatting to each other about the good ol' days while enjoying a cigarette made the waiting periods in between hunting pass very quickly.

Henry had a charismatic personality and people from all walks of life were drawn to him. His hunting buddies knew of his propensity to embellish and exaggerate, but his stories were fascinating. Once they fell under his spell, they thoroughly enjoyed his company.

After all, it could seem like an eternity crouched behind trees waiting for prey.

Henry O. Creque taking a quick break on a hunting excursion © Creque Family Archives

Shooting Competitions

Henry's brother-in-law, Leon, who is the author's grandfather, was treasurer of the rifle club and loved hunting and competing too. In 1936, he was credited with his *'splendid shooting'* in a competition with the USCG Marion team, coming from behind and rubbing more experienced shooters quite hard to capture first place. It was the highest one-match average yet made, 967.

My mother and her sister were not fond of hunting though. They felt sorry for the birds when their father sent them into the bush to pick them up, calling them, *'his little retrievers.'*

Scaly-Naped Pigeons

Scaly-Naped pigeons, also known as red-necked pigeons, were large, gray-colored birds, another family favorite. The maroon plumage around their necks had a scaly appearance, giving them their name.

By 1956, a license was needed, with hunting season open for a month and a half in October and November only.

When the *Virgin Islands National Park* was established in 1956, all hunting was forbidden within the Park boundaries. By the 1970s, the hunting laws changed outside the Park.

No more than ten Zenaida doves and five pigeons were allowed to be taken. The hunting of waterfowl, ground or quail doves or other pigeons was also prohibited.

The rifle club eventually disbanded, but all the members remained friends for a lifetime.

Catching Crabs

Near the Francis Bay home was a network of dirt holes where hundreds of crabs lived. At night, they crawled out of their secure burrows and scurried around from one hole to the next on a mission to nowhere.

The boys caught them using a flashlight, which temporarily blinded the crabs, stopping them in their tracks. They were quite skilled at scooping them up, wary of being snipped by their sharp pincers.

Tardy made a sweet crabmeat stew called *Carapacho,* which she served in the crabs' shells.

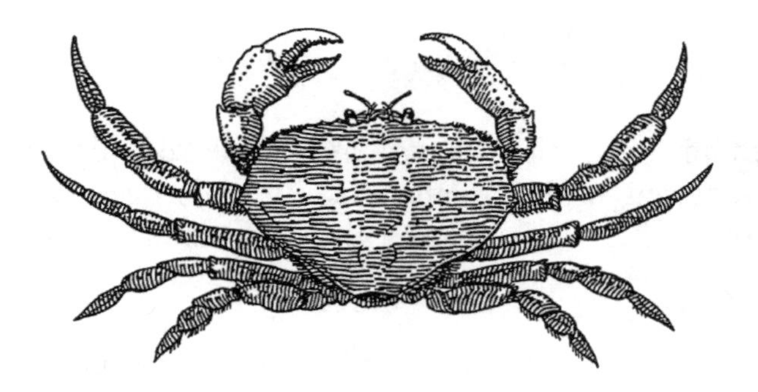

She kept a huge, metal cage to store them for at least a week while she fed them a cornmeal mixture to help purge them before preparing. This process rid the crab of anything unsanitary they may have eaten, essentially cleaning them from the inside.

At night, when the crabs were restless, the cage rattled as they clambered over each other, hitting the sides with their oversized claws, trying to escape.

As kids, my sister and I attempted to catch them by dipping long stalks of grass with a furry blossom at the end into the holes. It was so exciting to see a huge claw reach up from the muddy depths and latch on to our teaser. For us it was fun, but for our ancestors, it was a potential meal.

Cleaning the Crabs

To prepare her stew, Tardy cleaned the crabs first by dipping them into freshwater several times before she tossed them, legs facing down, into a pot of boiling ingredients. The water was flavored with hot Scotch Bonnet peppers, onions, Bay leaves, Garlic, and other seasonings. The shellbacks were cleaned too and later stuffed with the mixture, which included sautéed onions, peppers, and rice.

There wasn't anything Tardy couldn't make mouthwatering. This was one of her special gifts.

Crabbing from the Car

Richard Miller, an uncle, shared a funny story when he went crabbing at Magens Bay with two friends. They often went there after a heavy rain, encountering a sea of crabs on the sandy road. There must have been thousands of them, he said.

On one occasion, their friend, Mike Fuentes opened the driver's car door and grabbed one of the crabs and threw it into the back seat where Richard and another friend, Wayne Biggs, sat.

Richard Miller at Francis Bay, St. John © Creque Family Archives

It sent the two boys scrambling out of the back window in such a hurried attempt to escape that they almost landed on their heads! The laughter they shared was priceless.

Booby Eggs for Breakfast

My mother, her sister, Diane and their cousin Marion remembered how delicious brown booby eggs were when Tardy boiled them for breakfast.

The booby bird is a large, brown seabird with a white belly and webbed feet. In those days, they were commonly found along the thickets near the beach.

They laid their eggs in shallow nests dug into the dirt, and over time, would roll their eggs over and over to get them dirty, hoping to keep them better camouflaged from predators.

Although the yolk was more orange than a typical chicken's egg, my mother said, *they were very tasty.*

Combing the Seabed for Conch

Conch Stew, made with potatoes, onions, and tomatoes, was another delicious specialty Tardy prepared in the outdoor kitchen at Francis Bay. The boys combed the grassy seabed at Leinster Bay to collect them, diving in the shallows.

Processing the conch was not a fun job though. There's a special technique to extract the conch meat without destroying the shell. Despite the challenge, this dinner delicacy was enjoyed often and today is still a family favorite.

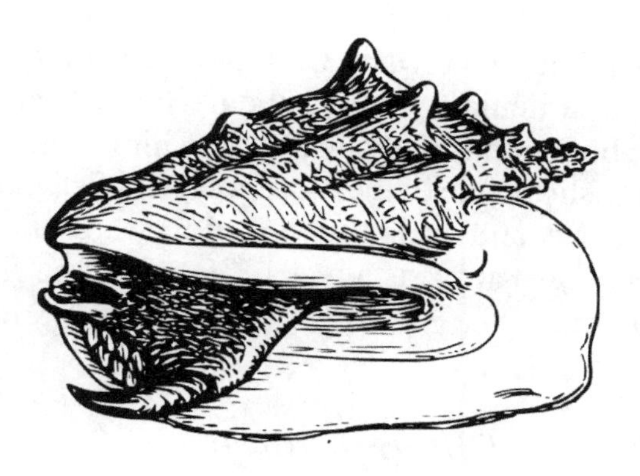

Finding Pink Pearls

Long ago—in 1906—a small, pink pearl was discovered in a conch shell by a St. Thomas fisherman when he began to scrape away the unusable parts. A grain of sand or another irritant must have lodged inside to create the pearl.

Word spread through the town and an eager buyer stepped forward with an offer of $6, which the finder accepted.

One was also found in the Bahamas years earlier in 1894, the *'finest ever brought to light.'* It was nearly as large as a pigeon's egg! Today, conch pearls in excellent condition can sell for as much as $15,000 per carat, but back then, the tasty meal was what was priceless.

Cooking Kingfish over a Coal-Pot

Herman was an avid sportsman and always wore khaki clothing and a pith helmet whenever he went fishing or hunting. His son-in-law, Arnold van Beverhoudt was his constant companion, along with one or two of the workmen.

One day, when the men went trolling, Herman caught a huge Kingfish he was particularly excited about. His sons gathered around to take a few photographs and congratulate him as he beamed from ear to ear. Kingfish are one of the most powerful fish in the sea. They were very delicious, and everyone looked forward to a scrumptious dinner that evening. Tardy, as always, knew just the right recipe to make it appetizing.

Filleting the Fish

She filleted the fish with a long, sharp knife, cut it into steaks and removed the red meat that ran down the centerline of the fish. Thyme, Garlic cloves, onions, salt, and pepper were crushed with an old marble mortar and pestle. The fish was sprinkled with fresh lime juice before Tardy grabbed a handful of the finely ground ingredients and lovingly smothered the portions deftly between her hands.

Into the cast-iron pan went a healthy chunk of Danish butter, then over the steaming coal pot it went. Within minutes, the fish took on a flavor that was out of this world! Oh, how everyone loved Tardy's cooking! Everything she cooked was mouthwatering! Tardy prepared all her meals with love.

Sometimes, the boys brought home yellowtail snappers, other times grouper. When the workmen went fishing, they preferred the catches from the fish pots that were baited, or a handline dropped over the reef. They caught gutu, redman, yellow jacks, blue runners or hardnose as they were known, and my mother's favorite, queen triggerfish, also known as '*ole wife*'.

A relative shared a silly story she had heard growing up of how parrotfish first became known as *gutu*. Shirley Gilker said, When God was naming all the fish, he didn't have a name for this type, so he said, *"You are good too"*, hence the name *gutu.* Fishing was thrilling and a necessary part of everyday life.

Herman O. Creque © Creque Family Archives

Arnold van Beverhoudt, Alphonse Harley and helper at Francis Bay © Creque Family Archives

Hunting for Goats at Mingo Cay ~ 1936

Herman was always looking for opportunities to expand his holdings. Like his father, he invested in property whenever he found an opportunity.

In 1936, he purchased the island of Mingo Cay, located in Pillsbury Sound between St. Thomas and St. John. According to tax records, it was a fifty-acre parcel known as, *23 Saint Senior Island.* He bought it from Alice Smith, a widow of Lovango Cay, for $800 on August 10, 1936.

The island was perfect for hunting excursions. Herman's son-in-law, Arnold, grand-son-in-law, Richard Miller and the foreman, Alphonse Harley went hunting there on many occasions.

Their catches were brought back to Francis Bay, hung up in the Flamboyant tree and cleaned before Tardy turned them into delectable dishes.

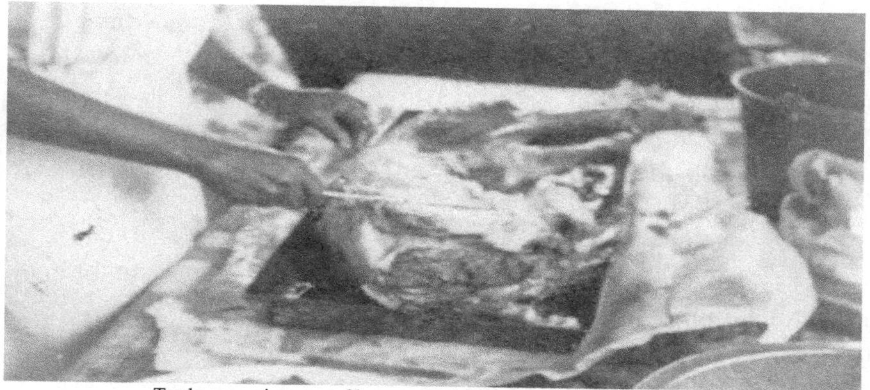

Tardy preparing one of her specialties © Creque Family Archives

Tardy's Delicious Dinners

Tardy was never squeamish about seeing or handling a fresh catch, whether they were birds, fish or other small animals.

She would gingerly remove the gunshot from the birds, feeling for the hard pellets between her fingers as she de-feathered them before seasoning and marinating.

She had help on occasions and taught her assistants how to prepare her delicious entrees. Her cookbook was filled with all of her delicacies! Thanks to Francis LeCuyer, a cousin who shared a copy of Tardy's recipes, we know what some of her specialties were.

Accompanying her dishes were either quick biscuits, banana nut bread, fish balls—which she made by passing the snapper through a meat grinder until fine—bread dumplings, papaya chutney, cinnamon cookies or rum pudding to name a few.

Gundy was another specialty Tardy excelled at. I watched her make it on several occasions. Using a metal meat grinder with a hand crank, she passed the smoked herring fillets through, then mixed it with potatoes, Scotch Bonnet peppers, olives, and beets. This gave the mixture a bright red color.

Gundy was eaten on Good Friday and throughout Lent when the family abstained from eating meat. Meals were sumptuous considering there was no running water, stove or electric freezer. What Tardy didn't bring from St. Thomas, she prepared with the coal pot or with the burning embers in the outdoor charcoal oven during the daylight hours.

Dinner meals were served early in the evening with kerosene lamps on the table, dining under the stars with a chorus of crickets and tree frogs singing to each other. It was the most memorable childhood anyone could wish for!

The *Chips* docked at the Creque Marine Railway © Creque Family Archives

Catching a Crevalle Jack

When Henry felt adventurous, he went trolling on the *Chips*, sometimes catching Crevalle Jacks on his rod for fun. They were a powerful, predatory fish that rarely refused anything they were offered. Henry and his brother Frank loved to hook them using shiny lures, but preferred fresh bait, like squid, when available.

Henry O. Creque with a Crevalle jack © Creque Family Archives

This one was likely caught a considerable distance from shore since the larger adults preferred deeper waters. These types of fish were found where the strong currents were likely to appear or where the seabed suddenly changed, like over a reef or ledge.

Although exciting to catch, jacks were considered poor table fare and were not consumed. Their red flesh was very dark due to their dense muscle, which made them coarse and terrible tasting! When pulled from the water, Crevalle's were known to snort in what many people described as a pig-like fashion.

These fun times together brought the family closer. Many of their fondest memories were spent on the boat or picnicking on the beach.

Market Day, Tortola, British Virgin Islands © Harvard University, Schlesinger Library

Shopping Trips to Tortola

Besides fishing, the family enjoyed boating excursions to nearby islands. Since, one day a week was designated as the shopping day, Herman gathered everyone for a boat trip to Road Town on '*Market day*'.

It was a direct run from Mary's Creek and a lot more fun to go to Tortola by boat for produce and ice, than to Cruz Bay by horse or donkey. It allowed Herman the opportunity to check on his properties. He owned a parcel in Road Town, which he rented, and eleven acres of *Threlfall's Estate* above Sea Cows Bay.

When they arrived, everyone dispersed to fill their baskets with pineapples, cassava, potatoes, yams, bananas, breadfruit, and more, as Herman tended to business matters.

My mother never accompanied them because she suffered terribly with seasickness. She stayed behind to play games with her cousins. Later, she would sit on the concrete cistern next to the house and keep a lookout for them in Mary's Creek. When she saw the *Chips* on the horizon, she ran to tell everyone that they were returning home!

The jetty at Norman Island, British Virgin Islands © Frederick Fenger

Norman Island, 1896 – 1999

Other boating excursions took the family to Norman Island, an island Herman's father purchased in 1896. Henry Osmond Creque acquired the property from Mrs. Hill, a widow of the former owner, for forty pounds sterling. The island had been sitting dormant for over fifty years.

Alexander LaFontaine, whom Herman knew from St. Thomas, was hired as an overseer in his absence. In 1937, they both worked together to make repairs to the small stone cottage on the beach. Herman brought twenty sheets of galvanized material on his boat along with wooden planks, iron nails, cement and tools to complete the job. Remarkably, the walls of this cottage still stand today.

Treasure Island

Norman Island was reputed to be the island Robert Louis Stevenson used as his inspiration for his classic book, *Treasure Island.* Since buried treasure was found on the island in 1750, its history has captured the imaginations of many. The island remained in the Creque family for 103 years, until it was sold in 1999.

Picking up Fish at Peter Island, 1913 - 1982

On other occasions, Herman took the family to Peter Island when he went to pick up fresh fish.

His father was the highest bidder for a parcel of sixty-three acres, which included the beach at Great Harbor. Henry paid $350 for the land at an auction. It once belonged to the children of Isaac Farrington but—in 1913—it was lost due to unpaid taxes.

Some years later, Henry lost it as well for the same reason, but repurchased the land in his business's name (*The Caribbean Coal and Fuel Company*) when it came up for auction again. He planned to build a coaling station there but passed away two years later, in 1915.

In 1934, his son also invested in the tiny island, purchasing twenty-six acres from Ethelfreida Titley for $100 and in 1937, he acquired fifty-four acres of Balsam Hill.

Henry O. Creque, Herman's son © Creque Family Archives

This brought Herman's ownership of Peter Island to 143 acres in total.

Since the property lay dormant over the years, Herman gave Alexander LaFontaine and his wife Estelle, permission to use his land surrounding the Great Harbor beach to haul, dry, and repair their fishing nets.

The area in front of the shallow beachfront, known as, *the Peter Island Bight*, was notorious for schooling sprat and was used for catching bait by *all* the fishermen in the British Virgin Islands.

The LaFontaine's had a unique arrangement with Herman. They paid their rent with buckets of fish.

Long after Herman passed away in 1949, and Alexander passed in 1978, Herman's heirs decided to sell the land they inherited to *Peter Island Resort, Ltd.*

In early 1980, Estelle claimed the beachfront property for herself. She filed a 'caution' with the *Registrar of Lands*, claiming her *'use of the Creque family's property since 1932 without permission.'*

No-one in the family ever went over to pick up any more fish after Herman died.

Consequently, over four acres of the beautiful beachfront acreage was subsequently lost when Estelle's BVI lawyer brought up the matter of, *adverse possession.*

Sadly, it would not be the last time the Creque family lost acres of land through this legal principle in the law.

Valerie Creque and her sister, Olga © Creque Family Archives

The Death of Olga Creque - van Beverhoudt

Just before Christmas 1942, as everyone was looking forward to the holidays, the family was devastated by the sudden death of one of their loved ones, a beautiful daughter, mother, wife, and sister.

Olga or Ollie as she was often called, passed away unexpectedly. She was Herman and Emily's eldest child and my grandmother, Val's sister and closest confidant. The two sisters shared a loving bond from the time they were two and four years old when they bathed in the same oversized wash pan every day.

As young girls, they loved playing with their Jenny Lind dolls, sitting them up for imaginary tea parties on the rooftop of their Main Street home. Later, as teenagers they confided in each other, often keeping secrets from their two brothers.

They attended the Convent School during the week and Catholic Mass every Sunday and were simply inseparable, even attending the *Holy Trinity School* in Puerto Rico, until marriage and having children took them in separate directions. Before Olga died, Val had a dream that something terrible was going to happen.

The Dream

At the time, Val was on a Christmas vacation in Puerto Rico, staying at her favorite place, the Palace Hotel. One evening, she dreamt she saw two horses pulling a cart with a coffin down the center of Main Street. Seated alongside the driver was her sister, Ollie.

She asked her, *"Who is it, Ollie, who is it?"*, curious to know who had died? *"Is it so and so? guessing a list of names."* Ollie shook her head, no. Val kept guessing and prodding her. *"Is it so and so?"* Again, Ollie shook her head, no.

When Val returned to St. Thomas, she was told the sorrowful news that her sister had died. Heartbroken, she didn't understand what could have happened. Ollie had given birth to a baby girl five weeks prior. She'd been happy and healthy when she left on her trip.

In those days, it was customary to stay in bed for a long time, even weeks, after the birth of a baby. Sadly, Ollie had developed a blood clot while recuperating that subsequently traveled to her heart. She was thirty-three years old and a mother to three small girls, Marion, Joanie, and the new baby, Jackie Rose.

The grief Val felt was overwhelming. Ollie had been her best friend, and she didn't have the opportunity to say goodbye. Her obituary announcement was published on December 21, 1942, in *The Virgin Islands Daily News* and read:

"Mrs. Henrietta Olga van Beverhoudt, a member of one of St. Thomas' most prominent families, died at her home at 10:25 yesterday morning, after an illness of two weeks. She was 33 years of age. Daughter of Mr. and Mrs. Herman O. Creque, and wife of Mr. Arnold van Beverhoudt, Mrs. van Beverhoudt has a month ago given birth to her third child."

As a tribute, Val wrote the following poem.

My Sister

Poems from A Small Island
Written about Olga by her sister
© Valerie Creque-Mawson

You were sleeping, sister, sleeping...
And you smiled a happy smile...
As I called to you while weeping
Like a brokenhearted child.

So, I sadly bent to kiss you,
Placed a rose within your hand,
and I whispered:
"Dearest, how we'll miss you....
More than you can understand.

Did you hear me, sister, hear me
When I called to you that day?
Do you sometimes linger near me
As I go along my way?

You were sleeping, sister sleeping,
With your face serene and calm;
But I knew though I was weeping,
You were safe in Jesus' arms.

For I know that life is fleeting,
When I draw that one last breath,
We'll be meeting, sister meeting
Far beyond the doors of death.

In that land that God has given;
In that great Eternity,
In that afterworld called Heaven,
Where dwells Immortality. †

The Dream of Another Dimension

Months later, Val had another unusual dream. While she was sleeping, she suddenly became aware that she was somewhere else. She said it felt like another dimension. As she looked about, she recognized her sister with a group of people just a short distance away. Suddenly, Ollie came towards her, and she ran to embrace her. *"Ol, do you know that you have passed?"*, Val asked.

Ollie nodded her head and answered, *"Yes Val, I know." "Ol, are you happy? Are you happy, Ol?" Val inquired.*

"If it's just to stop you asking these questions, yes Val, I'm happy", Ollie replied. Then she said something profound that Val never forgot.

Ollie told her, *"Val, you'll never begin to know the structure of things."*

Just then, a woman from the group approached the sisters and asked Val, "What are you doing here? Go back. How did you get here? You shouldn't be here." Shortly afterward, Val woke up.

The Death of Valerie Creque-Mawson
St. John ~ 2002

When Val passed away sixty years later, my mother and I were sitting by her bedside holding her hands.

Moments before she died, she looked up toward the foot of the bed and my mom noticed how bright and clear her eyes were, as if she recognized someone who had come to greet her.

We had a distinct feeling it was her beloved sister, returning to take her home.

Marlene

Chapter 8

My Mother's Memories of Mary's Point 1940s

To Herman and Emily's granddaughter, Francis Bay was the most beautiful beach in the world! Some of her fondest childhood memories were spent there with them. This is my mom's story, in her own words of a very special time in her life.

Herman and Frank Creque at the waterfront dock with the *M/V Chips* © Creque Family Archives

Annual Sojourns to St. John

"Every June, our family packed the necessary supplies and foodstuffs in preparation for our annual sojourn from St. Thomas to St. John.

My grandfather owned the Creque Department Store on Main Street and the building extended backward to the waterfront with its own private wharf. Because of rough weather, his boat was kept at Hassel Island at the railway and brought over when needed.

Accompanying us on our trip was my grandmother, my sister Diane; cousins Marion and Joan, as well as their dad, Arnold. The girls ranged in age from six to twelve years old.

Our beloved nanny, Tardy came with us too. Everyone scrambled aboard grandfather's favorite boat to get a good seat. It was called the *Chips*. All five of his boats started with the letter "C" for Creque.

Before heading out, I watched in anticipation as the workmen loaded the kerosene stove. They continued until all the boxes for the summer-long stay were stored below. It was a very exciting time for me, however, I was not looking forward to the boat ride at all! I was the only one in the family susceptible to motion sickness.

Curing Motion Sickness

On this particular day, the seas were quite choppy, so it made the ride seem longer than usual. Thankfully, Tardy had thought to bring along a few fresh leaves from the lime tree in our yard. These, she crushed in her hand and gave to me to smell. This made me feel a lot better.

Somehow, Tardy always knew exactly what to do in every situation. It was so good to have her around, no matter what the day might bring.

The Slave Rocks

When we neared Mary's Point, my grandfather pointed out the red rocks on the cliff, called *Slave Rocks*.

He told us the story about a number of slaves that escaped, and rather than being caught and enslaved again, jumped to their deaths. He said, *'it forever stained the rocks a crimson color.'*

This story left such a lasting impression on me as a young girl, that it was never forgotten.

Arriving in Mary's Creek

As we reached the calm and sheltered bay of Mary's Creek, my grandfather blew the boat's horn and John, the estates caretaker, rowed out to greet us. He always beamed when he saw *The Boss*, as he respectfully called my grandfather.

The *M/V Chips* arriving in Mary's Creek, St. John, US Virgin Islands © Creque Family Archives

We were delighted to finally arrive and quickly jumped into John's dinghy for the short ride to shore. From the beach, we walked up the trail toward our quaint, but familiar summer home.

We passed John's small, stone cottage to our left, and then came upon the corral where many of the cows were kept. You could hear them mooing as we approached!

As the house came into view, the girls and I started running toward the front door, trying to be the first to enter and claim our coveted sleeping spots.

The Francis Bay Home

Our family home was a stone's throw from the beach on a winding rocky trail flanked by large crab holes. It had been built many years prior but was painted and enclosed with fencing soon after its purchase.

There was a huge lime tree next to the cistern that produced the juiciest limes. It had probably been a transplant from *Lamesure Estate* when they were cultivating lime trees for export.

Milking the Cows

The next morning, we decided to get up very early to see the cows being milked. My uncle, Arnold wanted to experience this too and to taste the milk straight from the cow. I was not that adventurous! Besides, I never liked milk and didn't care to taste it.

Every morning, John milked the cows and brought a pitcher up to the house. Tardy placed it on the stove in the old stone kitchen and boiled it. We asked why, and Tardy remarked, *"it has to be scalded first before it can be drunk."*

We were amazed to see a thin, hardened layer of cream form on the top. Tardy delicately lifted this off and threw it away. After boiling, the milk smelled like slightly burnt marshmallows.

Early Morning Walks

Each day, we accompanied Grampoo, as we lovingly called our grandfather, on his early morning walk and swim down to Francis Bay beach.

Along the winding trail, we passed a marshy area in the mangroves where lots of big crabs lived in huge holes. The area had a strange, earthy smell we didn't like.

A short distance farther, the beach opened up before us, so pristine and beautiful. We loved swimming there! We ran and splashed each other, enjoying the feel of the cool water on our sun-warmed skin. Grandmother never accompanied us on these walks. She preferred to stay behind on the shaded, tiled verandah, enjoying a cup of tea.

Many of our walks took us towards Leinster Bay. We walked mostly in the water, stopping to collect whelks that adhered to the rocks or pretty shells we found in the shallows.

There was an overgrown trail through the *Annaberg* ruins that we avoided. We did not want to climb through the brush and risk getting caught by the catch 'n' keep.

Back then, we never feared someone would harm us because no one was ever around. We often marveled that Grampoo owned, *'as far as our eyes could see.'*

Delightful Donkey Rides

When not exploring the shoreline, we played cards and jumped rope under the big, shady trees. We particularly enjoyed prying open the large, green pods we picked and were delighted to see an unusually small, white, bird-like form inside.

Sometimes, we even ventured for a donkey ride. John lifted us into the wooden boxes strapped to the donkey's sides and reminded us to hold on tightly.

My sister, Diane was crouched in one box and I was in the other. We screamed with delight as we bounced around while the donkey trotted madly along the trail. It was a carefree time, full of laughter and fun!

Dinner Time

I remember the dining room where we all met for dinner at the end of the day. At a large mahogany table, lit by kerosene lamps on either end, everyone had their assigned seats.

On the sideboard to the left were thin, crystal glasses for everyday use. The kids often enjoyed fresh limeade made from the limes of the tree that grew near the cistern.

Our meals were varied and delicious, thanks to Tardy, of course.

For breakfast, we enjoyed hard-boiled Booby eggs. The whites were translucent, while the yolk was much more intensely yellow, almost a deep orange compared to a chicken's egg. They were very delicious.

For dinner, we sometimes ate stewed mountain doves. On the other nights, it may have been venison or whatever else was freshly caught.

Once, I even tried turtle soup for the first time. Dumb bread though, was still my favorite staple.

Henry Ogilvie Creque, (1912 – 1957) © Creque Family Archives

Hunting for Goats

On many occasions, Grampoo and my Uncle Arnold went hunting for goats. When they returned one day from their explorations, we discovered they had caught one and hung it in the Flamboyant tree in the front yard. It was to be divided up and shared for meat, but we were too squeamish to watch the process.

Folklore Tales

After supper one night, we went out to the verandah to find our grandparents sitting in two wooden armchairs. I sat with the other girls on the stone steps leading up to the front porch and waited with great anticipation.

We loved to hear John's West Indian folklore tales. He entertained us with scary stories about two spiders, *Bru Anansi,* and *Bru Takoma.*

The evening was dark and the sounds of the crickets and tree frogs calling sent shivers down our spines. Even the Mountain doves were cooing.

We asked John as we huddled together, *"What are the doves saying?"* to which he replied with a smile. *"When they make their calls, they say, 'Father God, send rain'."*

Although the home sits in ruins today, my happy memories linger on."

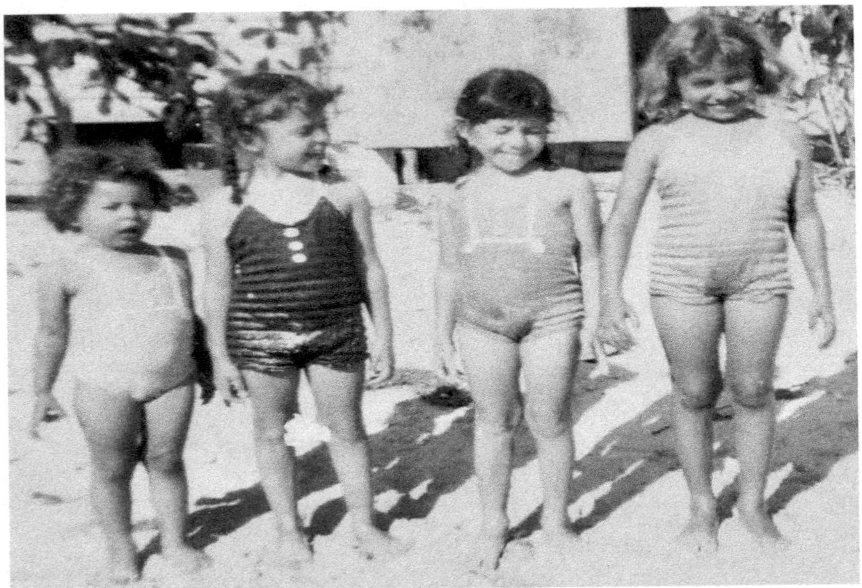

Joan, Diane, Marlene and Marion © Creque Family Archives

Chapter 9

The Original Idea for The Virgin Islands National Park

Governor Pearson's Invitation

The original idea for the establishment of a National Park on St. John may have come as early as 1934 under the guidance of Governor Paul M. Pearson.

On June 1, Governor Pearson returned to St. Thomas from a visit to Washington DC, where he had been discussing the island's legislation with lawmakers.

National Park Officials Visit ~ 1934

Accompanying him on his return flight were two officials from the National Park Service, Dr. Harold C. Bryant, the Assistant Director, and George M. Wright. They were looking over the gardens, parks and other beautiful spots in St. Thomas to improve and develop them. Mr. R. Watson, a field examiner with the Civil Works Administration, was also in attendance and was surveying the activities of the local C.W.A.

On June 2, 1934, all three visitors were entertained at Government House before embarking on a special visit to St. John on Saturday afternoon for a closer look around.

Touring St. John by Boat

According to a passage in Governor Pearson's diary, the group *'rode entirely around the island by boat so that the men of the National Park Service could get an idea of it.'*

They returned to the Battery at the end of the day and spent the evening on the balcony, enjoying the wonderful views of the sky and sea, *'one of the most outstanding scenes of the Virgin Islands'*.

The trails of St. John © The Royal Library of Denmark, Lars Peter Elfelt, Photographer

Trotting Through the Trails

By 7:30 a.m. Sunday morning, they were all in the saddle and headed out for a 6 ½-hour ride through the beautiful trails of St. John. Governor Pearson wanted to show them around himself, having toured the island by horseback two months prior.

Their riding trip took them to the highest peak, *Bordeaux Mountain*, where the best bay trees were grown and then back to the Centerline Road and to *Annaberg Estate*, returning on the north side to Little Cruz Bay.
'This was one of the finest trails any visitor has ever been over,' Governor Pearson wrote. Honorable Creque very likely met the group at the top of *Bordeaux* to explain the bay tree industry further.

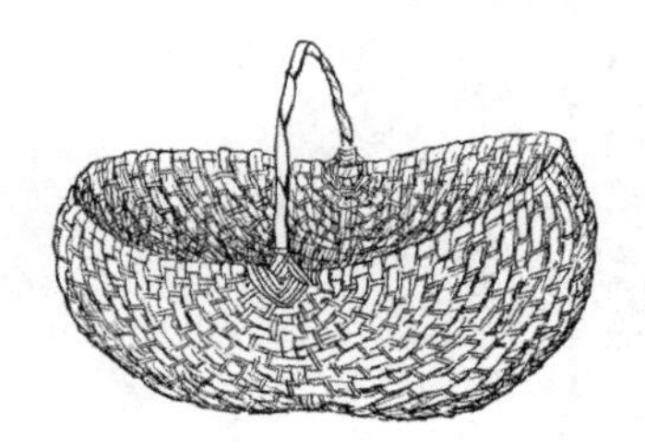

Best to Develop the Basketry and Bay Oil Industry

Despite having one of the *'finest times anybody ever had'*, Governor Pearson felt that *nothing* would probably come of the National Park idea for St. John.

He learned that *'once a property met the requirement of being something most unusual that could be greatly enjoyed by the people, no commercial enterprise of any kind would be permitted and all the people who live in the area would be deported.'*

This was an unsettling revelation…

To Governor Pearson, it seemed much wiser to keep the line of development they were on, which was to develop the bay oil, basketry, and homesteading industries, and then add the development of hotels and rental cottages for tourists. *'I do not know just how we are to manage this, but we will find a way. The things that ought to be done, somehow get done, if there is somebody who is convinced that they should be done and is willing to take the gaff in getting them accomplished.'*

Harold Hubler and Conrad Wirth © Virgin Islands National Park

Harold A. Hubler ~ 1937

According to the inaugural booklet for the *Virgin Islands National Park*, a ranger was credited with being the first to dream of a National Park on St. John. His name was Hal Hubler. He began his career as a graduate landscape architect.

'Back in 1937, when jobs were very scarce, Hal was sent to the Virgin Islands to be in charge of camps for men who needed work. Their job was to repair forests that were beginning to decay.

'Two years later, Hal wrote a report to the Department of the Interior, urging that the St. John forest be permanently preserved as a park. Shortly after, World War II broke out and nobody in Washington had any time to think about parks anymore.

'Fifteen years later, Hal Hubler's telephone rang in Omaha, Nebraska. On the other end of the wire was the Director of the National Park Service in Washington DC, Conrad Wirth. He asked Hal if he would like to go back to St. John to see if he still thought a park there would be a good idea. Mr. Rockefeller had offered to buy and donate the land.'

The Hubler Report ~ 1939

In 1939, Hal Hubler sent his report about the little island of St. John that he believed to be by far, *'the most beautiful of the three US Virgin Islands'* to the Department of the Interior.

One extract reads:

'The pure white sand of her north side beaches made a perfect contrast between the green of her wooded hills and the turquoise waters washing her shores.

'At no place in the Sir Francis Drake channel is the water very deep, hence the ocean floor with all its beauties and wonders can be seen through the clear waters.

'Rainbow-hued fish swim in lazy abandon, sea fans of deep purple grow from the coral bottom, and sea anemones with petal-like fronds wave to and fro on the water currents, luring unsuspecting animals.

'Nowhere does the sun set in such an array of ever-changing glory.'

The almost forty-page report continued to describe the island's historical features, general characteristics, hotel, and guest house accommodations as well as the marine life.

He highlighted the activities guests would love spending time doing, like hiking, riding, fishing, swimming, relaxing and stargazing, *'for the stars shine with amazing brilliance.'*

It's uncertain if Hal Hubler was aware of earlier visits by National Park representatives, but later that year, the new governor extended an invitation of his own to Park officials.

Governor Cramer's Invitation ~ 1939

While visiting Washington DC, Governor Lawrence Cramer invited senior National Park officials to visit the islands.

He did this with the hope of *'rekindling their acquaintance with the Virgin Islands to see what was being done by Municipal and Federal governments in preserving the scenic, historic, scientific and recreational features of the islands.'*

Governor Lawrence Cramer and visiting dignitary © The Library of Congress

Dr. Francis Ronalds, Chief of the Division of Historic Sites from the National Park Service in Washington DC, and George L. Collins, Assistant Regional Director from Santa Fe, New Mexico, arrived in December of 1939.

'In the company of Harold A. Hubler, Supervisor of the local CCC Camp, the group visited St. John. Both were impressed by the island's beauty and the *'traditional courtesy and happiness of the people.'*

Nothing would come of these visits, however, since World War II intervened, lasting from September 1, 1939, to September 2, 1945.

Committee Members visit St. John ~ 1952

By 1952, the war was over and there was a new governor for the Virgin Islands, Morris Fidanque de Castro. He entertained members from the *Committee on Interior and Insular Affairs*, taking them on a visit to St. John when interest was renewed.

The following month, in February 1952, he met with the Chairman of the *Advisory Board of the National Park Service* while he was on the island vacationing.

It wasn't until Frank Stick wrote a letter in 1954 to the then Governor, Archibald Alexander, proposing a National Park for St. John, that things began to happen.

Frank Stick's Correspondence with Laurance Rockefeller ~ May 30, 1954

According to Bruce Schoonover's research, after Frank wrote to Governor Alexander, he also wrote to Laurance Rockefeller.

In his letter to him, he referenced *Hubler's 1939 Report* for the possibility of a National Park for St. John.

The rest, as they say….*is history*.

A view of Francis Bay, St. John © Valerie Sims, Creque Family Archives

The Sale of Francis Bay ~ 1954

By the summer of 1954, Frank Stick was working with Laurance Rockefeller on securing lands for inclusion in the new National Park they envisioned for the island.

Frank Stick approached Emily again, regarding an *option* to purchase *Estates Annaberg, Francis Bay, Mary's Point* and *Concordia*. She agreed and signed a *binder contract* shortly thereafter. The two had met previously when she sold *Lamesure Estate* to him.

It's uncertain whether she'd been aware of Mr. Rockefeller's plans when she agreed to sell her properties, as both his involvement and his park plans were not made public until months later.

Expanding Caneel Bay ~ 1954

According to the *New York Times* of November 19, 1954, Mr. Rockefeller had already spent a substantial sum in developing Caneel Bay, accommodating forty-eight guests.

The hotel was being doubled in size, and a new sewer system and power plant were being installed, as well as a water-catchment and new employee quarters. The dock was being enlarged, the road system established, and extensive landscaping of the shore was planned.

In late November, *The Virgin Islands Daily News* began publishing a series of articles supporting Mr. Rockefeller's Park plans. The below feature was the first of three articles and may have been the first time St. John residents and property owners became aware of his Park idea.

Rockefeller offers USA, a Virgin Islands Park

He Seeks to Preserve the Unspoiled Beauty of St. John Paradise

*

No Resident to be Displaced

The Virgin Islands Daily News ~ November 20, 1954

~ By Morris Kaplan

Laurance Rockefeller, Conrad L. Wirth, Director of the National Park and Frank Stick spent five days on St. John.

According to this article, Mr. Rockefeller had acquired options to purchase about half of the scenic island. It went on to quote how he found *'the combination of mountains, beaches, and sea unique in the Caribbean. The unspoiled nature of the area appealed to me and I wish to preserve it against overdevelopment.'*

Rockefeller was disturbed that the most beautiful areas of St. John might someday be altered to destroy their natural beauty.

Should a National Park be approved, he said, *it would not displace anyone. 'It would allow for the natural expansion and development of the settlement areas of Coral Bay and Cruz Bay and would not, in any way, adversely affect the livelihood of the seven hundred persons on the island.'*

Arriving at the Caneel Bay Dock © Creque Family Archives

A Natural Park for St. John

The Virgin Islands Daily News ~ November 22, 1954

According to this second article published two days later, *'Some people might be misled into the belief that the residents will be placed in a less favorable position by this development.*

As we see it, it is the most fortunate thing that has happened to St. John in several decades.

'The development of the natural park would bring new activity to the small island and improve the economic condition by attracting a better type of visitor.

'We hope that the administration and the legislature will cooperate fully in bringing about this most significant development for the benefit of the entire Virgin Islands.'

Laurance Rockefeller and his wife, Mary © John Bottega, The Library of Congress (1965)

The following day, the third article appeared which further embellished Mr. Rockefeller's position.

Mr. Rockefeller's Fine Offer

The Virgin Islands Daily News ~ November 23, 1954

'The island appears from every account to be an incomparable spot of bliss and beauty.

This is the bit of paradise in the Virgin Islands that has won the heart of Mr. Laurance S. Rockefeller so completely, that he wants to give a large part of St. John to the American people for a National Park. Having fallen in love with St. John, he wants the entire nation to share in the delight.

It's easy to understand why this island excites ecstasy.'

- *'There are green mountains, white beaches, and seas of the purest turquoise.*
- *The place is unspoiled; it has a history that goes back to Columbus.*
- *The island is covered with trees in tropical richness and ringed by beaches of extraordinary beauty.*
- *The climate is practically perfect. St. John offers everything that the tourist could wish for.*
- *There is every reason that St. John should be preserved for the enjoyment of the nation.*
- *Such regions of felicity, where nature's enchantments are so uniquely combined, are only too rare.'*

'It is to be hoped that the Department of the Interior will make an enthusiastic recommendation to Congress and that Mr. Rockefeller's offer will be quickly accepted with the vote of thanks from all the people.'

(*The New York Herald-Tribune*, republished in *The Virgin Islands Daily News,* November 23, 1954).

Olga Creque, her sister, Val, a friend, and their aunt, Florelia Cid, 1930s © Creque Family Archives

The Unthinkable Loss of Francis Bay

December 30, 1954

By November, Frank Stick transferred his option contract on the *Mary's Point/Francis Bay* land, including the *Estates of Annaberg and Concordia* to *Jackson Hole Preserve, Inc.*, Laurance Rockefeller's company.

They followed through and finalized the purchase with Emily directly. She signed the deed on December 30, 1954, with her attorney, Cyril E. Michael, and Leo Penha as witnesses.

Seven hundred acres, possibly more, of pristine coastline, historic ruins and her children's favorite beach cottage at Francis Bay were included.

Emily kept this transaction ***a secret*** from her five adult children.

They had no idea she had sold the family estates!

She never discussed it with them beforehand, and no one close to her understood why she would do something like that without ever mentioning it. Her children wondered whether she had been told not to say anything about who was really purchasing the property. All the siblings did know was that overnight, their favorite summer home was gone! All the amazing times spent there were now only memories.

Emily's decision caused incredible heartache and divided the family. Surely, she knew what Francis Bay meant to her children? They had spent almost thirty years of their lives on the beach; laughing, having fun, and making memories. One day, the beach and cottage would be theirs to pass to their children to make their own special memories, or so they thought.

When her eldest son found out what his mother had done, he was *'extremely irate and upset'*. Henry was a senator in St. Thomas and could have assisted or advised her on the best course of action. He was convinced she had been persuaded to sell because he felt that *'Rockefeller wanted to protect his interests at Caneel Bay by preventing others from developing their lands.'* He was also angry because he believed that she did not receive the true value for her estates. He said that, *'Mary's Point alone was worth a million dollars!'*

Henry refused to speak with his mother ever again over her decision. In fact, he wanted to legally declare her *mentally incompetent*, but his sister was adamantly against this and argued with him until he acquiesced. Val's pride would never have allowed him to proceed. This tore the family apart with each sibling taking a different position. Henry was not the only one devastated by the news. Val was especially saddened and felt betrayed. She was her mother's closest confidant.

That Christmas season, each of Emily's children received checks in their Christmas cards, a bittersweet bonus they were not expecting. Instead of being happy, they were heartbroken.

Disillusionment

Poems from A Small Island

When I was a child…in the years that are past,
I looked at the world through a rose-colored glass.
A world that was rosy…and happy and bright,
All bathed by my dreams…in a soft golden light.

But now, I have found, as I look through the years,
My rose-colored glass is all streaked with tears.
The rose on my glass has all worn away,
My dreams are all broken…my world is all gray.

Facing the truth… my heart cries in vain,
Oh… if I were, but a child once again.

Laurance Rockefeller passing the St. John deeds to Secretary Seaton, Cruz Bay © 1956, Sam Falk

The Dedication Ceremony ~ 1956

The dedication ceremony for the new *Virgin Islands National Park* took place on December 1, 1956, in Cruz Bay.

Thirty-five leading newspapermen, TV and radio commentators were flown down from New York to cover the Park's dedication. Rockefeller presented the title to more than 5,000 acres of land on St. John to the Federal government for the establishment of the twenty-ninth, US National Park.

'In keeping with the family tradition of grants and endowments on a prodigious level, Laurance S. Rockefeller gave to the nation a ***$4,000,000.00 gift*** *of sylvan woodlands, beaches and picturesque heights of natural, untrammeled beauty.'*

(*The Virgin Islands Daily News*, December 4, 1956)

Interestingly, *Jackson Hole Preserve, Inc.* paid $962,100 for the 5,086 acres, which equated to approximately $189.00 per acre.

Could the value of the properties have skyrocketed to four million dollars in the two years since Laurance Rockefeller had been acquiring them?

Henry didn't believe so. Reading about *'Rockefeller's gift to the nation'* in the newspaper only strengthened his position that his mother's properties were worth more than she had received.

Coincidentally, Caneel Bay Plantation opened its newly renovated hotel *on the same day* of the dedication ceremony for the new Park. (*The Virgin Islands Daily News*, December 1, 1956)

Henry was not happy.

Emily's Lands Become 42% of New National Park

Emily's decision to sell her lands would not have hurt her children so deeply had she discussed the matter with them first. Perhaps they could have agreed to keep the Francis Bay home they adored, and the surrounding acreage.

Now, all the properties were gone as Laurance Rockefeller was expanding and doubling the size of *his* property.

Incredibly, Emily had once owned ***forty-two percent*** (2,100+ acres) of the lands that made up the new *Virgin Islands National Park*, which at that time was 5,086 acres.

Henry was angry and bitter. He never returned to St. John again, nor discussed the matter with his wife. In the sixty years that Peggy lived on St. Thomas, she never once visited St. John.

Frank Stick's Perspective ~ November 10, 1954

According to a prospectus prepared by Frank on Emily's properties, the *Mary's Point/Francis Bay* tract was considered *'the most valuable estate on St. John.'*

- It was the finest location, and from the standpoint of topography and scenic beauty, the most perfect site for an outstanding hotel or cottage development.

- It was the only spot on the Atlantic side of St. John which had a safe harbor under any weather conditions and unaffected by the groundswell from the Atlantic.

- While rugged on the north from the landward side, the terrain shelved gradually upward to a height of 578 feet above sea level.

- The setting was perhaps more tropical than any in the Virgin Islands, with groves of coconut and other palms, and jutting out as it does from the mainland, it received the benefit of breezes from each direction.

- The land was well grassed and had been used extensively for grazing yet had an abundant and interesting forest growth.

- Estimated at 250 Danish acres, the actual plot measurement showed it contained closer to 448 American acres with a good beach."

Estate Annaberg

Estate Annaberg, while without the unusual features of *Mary's Point* included mountain peaks up to 1,000 feet, was well-forested, had excellent grazing sections, and an interesting water frontage with beaches.

'It was in this area, according to history and tradition, that the embattled slaves, who had overthrown their masters in 1733, made their final stand against the imported French soldiers.

Some 300 men, women, and children, in preference to capture, threw themselves to destruction from the high promontory of Mary's Point. This legend, if indeed, legend it was, still affected the native population to the extent that they shunned this particular spot.

Estate Concordia

Section A of *Concordia*, which adjoined Lamesure, was high and mountainous, with one peak over 900 feet. It had excellent exposure and a vista that took in the British Islands. A single wedge of land extended to *Concordia Bay*. The area of these four tracts, (Emily Creque's properties) while indicated as 700 acres more or less, measured more than 1,000 American acres.

Frank Stick's View of Why Emily Creque Sold

Frank had an option contract for $260,000, the highest price which would be paid for any land on St. John. He was able to procure an option on Emily's properties, *'only because, following the death of her husband, she desired to settle the estate.'*

Interestingly, Herman's estate was settled and adjudicated to Emily as his sole heir and devisee on September 18, 1950. It was registered at the *Office of the Recorder of Deeds* two years before Frank arrived on the island. Emily had been receiving income from all of her husband's businesses and rental properties and had funds available if she wished to disburse any. It's uncertain why Frank said '*settling the estate'* was the reason for her selling.

To this day, no one in the family knows why she sold.

Leon A. Mawson, Marlene's father and the author's grandfather © Mawson Family Archives

Mawson Proposes Program for People of St. John

The Virgin Islands Daily News ~ October 2, 1962

Henry's brother-in-law became resentful too. Leon A. Mawson was married to Emily's daughter, Val, the author's grandmother. At the time, my grandfather was a Republican candidate-at-large, running for a seat in the legislature.

He was hurt by his mother-in-law's decision to sell Francis Bay without telling anyone and proposed a *'very bold and imaginative two-point program'* as a solution.

He told 350 registered voters that if he were elected, he would immediately *'contact Mr. Rockefeller and every Republican Congressman to persuade the Federal Government to abandon the National Park and restore eighty percent of its holding to the local government.'*

Forty percent of the land would be sold to St. Johnians in one to ten-acre lots for truck farming. The remainder would be committed to an industrialization program that would *'change the entire economy of St. John.'* My grandfather felt the National Park was a failure.

'Instead of bringing greater financial benefits, it took away the bread and butter from the poor man's table. It cut off his right to set his fish traps and denied him the use of the waterways, which he had enjoyed for centuries.' (*The Virgin Islands Daily News*, October 2, 1962)

He emphasized that their very inheritance had been taken from them. Now that the lands had become a protected park, they were no longer allowed to hunt or fish as they had done all their lives.
(*The Virgin Islands Daily News,* July 11, 1957, *No Hunting or Bearing Firearms in National Park*)

Residents Disillusioned ~ 1962

Residents became further disillusioned when the Federal Government sought additional lands namely: Grass Cay, Congo Bay, Carvel Rock, Whistling Cay, Stevens Cay, Cocoloba Cay, Booby Rock, and Le Duck, in August 1962, and when they wanted to condemn an additional 3,300 acres by *Eminent Domain* to complete their 9,000-acre park goal.

"The people have become a little bit emotional about the issue," Stewart Udall, the Secretary of the Interior said, *"but their feelings are not based on the facts."*

"The people are acting as though this is a revolutionary proposal, whereas condemnation, is part of a long-held Park policy." (*The Virgin Islands Daily News*, September 13, 1962)

Congressman J.T. Rutherford, Chairman of the House Sub-Committee, said he would offer an amendment to delete the V.I. Park bill relating to land condemnation that was before the Congress.
(*The Virgin Islands Daily News*, September 8, 1962)

Residents were not, however, averse to the clause that would allow the Federal Government to condemn five or six submerged offshore lands to *'protect the flora and fauna of the vast coral reefs adjoining the island'*.

Senator Moorehead Goes to Washington DC 1962

Senator Theovald Moorehead

Theovald E. Moorehead, a well-respected senator on St. John went to Washington DC to fight against the legislation that would permit federal condemnation of private property for National Park purposes. (*The Virgin Islands Daily News*, September 18, 1962)

According to former Senator-at-Large, Cleone Creque, Senator Moorehead, known locally as Mooie, never held back his opinions.

'He was a humble, conservative, family-oriented man who always put St. John first.'

Senator Cleone Creque

Mooie and others were upset that the Park wanted to include an additional fifty-three privately owned parcels, which consisted of 3,300 acres. Of the fifty-three parcels, thirty-three belonged to native-born St. Johnians, Moorhead said.

Residents of St. John hoped Congressman Rutherford's amendment concerning, *'deleting the power to condemn'*, would be successful.

Four days later, *The Virgin Islands Daily News* reported that *'Mooie Moorehead returned a hero to his constituents'*. (September 22, 1962)

This matter continues to be a heated issue, even today, for some families who remember the events as they unfolded.

Landowners Whose Property Became The Virgin Islands National Park, 1953-1956

1953

- Mrs. Emily Creque – Sold Estate Lamesure and others to Frank Stick and his partners, however, the deed reflected his son's name. (David Stick and his wife, Phyllis) David was acting as a '*strawman*' for his father. – 1,437+ acres. Frank Stick and his associates transferred these lands to Jackson Hole Preserve, Inc. two years later.

1954

- Mrs. Emily Creque – Sold Estate Annaberg, Mary's Point/Francis Bay and Estate Concordia to Frank Stick as an *option,* which was later transferred and finalized by Jackson Hole Preserve, Inc. – 719+ acres.

1955

- Frank R. Faulk – 651 acres, Reef Bay Estate
- Halvar Neptune Richards – 54 acres, Estate Susannaberg
- Irving J. Backer – 374 acres, Est Mollendal & Little Reef Bay
- Claudia Joshua – 150 acres, Estate Concordia – Ram's Head
- Julius Sprauve – 211 acres, Est. Sieben, Fish Bay, 14 acres
- Herbert E. Lockhart Dev. Corp – 843 acres, Estates Brown Bay, Hermitage & Mt. Pleasant Retreat, Haulover Bay, Turner's Point & Leinster Bay

1956

- Rafe Hartwell Boulon – 59.2 acres, Estate Trunk Bay
- Agnes and John Butler – 57 acres, No. 2 Estate Catherinberg
- Julia Chanler Laurin – 40 acres, No. 4. Estate Catherinberg
- Gerhardt Sprauve – 39 acres, Estate Adrian
- Laurance Rockefeller – 421 acres, Caneel Bay
- Colonel Leonard and Mrs. Sylvia Cox – 17.2 acres, Estate Haulover, aka/ Mitchell Point

Henry O. Creque, Jr., 1912 – 1957 © Creque Family Archives

The Death of Henry O. Creque ~ 1957

Three years passed by since Henry's mother sold the Francis Bay home and surrounding estates, and he still had not spoken with her. As her seventy-third birthday approached, his wife persuaded him to visit and wish her a Happy Birthday. Peggy thought it was *'time to break the silence and put the past behind them'*.

On that fateful Saturday morning in May 1957, five months after the official ceremony in Cruz Bay transferring the deeds, they were sitting at a popular coffee shop on Radatts Gade, sharing a cup of coffee before the day's errands.

Henry finally conceded and bought a bouquet from the flower shop next door, then walked the short distance through Creque's Alley to the steps that led upstairs to where his mother resided. Peggy continued down Main Street to do some morning shopping.

Sadly, Henry never had the chance to speak with his mother again. As he walked through the inner alley, his chest tightened, and it became difficult for him to breathe. Within minutes, his knees buckled under him and he collapsed, gasping for breath. He suffered a massive heart attack close to the stairwell that led to his mother's residence. He was forty-four years of age.

Tardy saw him from the balcony above and ran to the telephone to call Dr. MacDonald and the ambulance right away. When she returned, she noticed that two Catholic nuns, passing in the alley, had stopped to offer assistance. They asked Tardy to quickly find a candle, so she ran back upstairs and called out to Miss Marion to tell her that something had happened to Mr. Henry. She then grabbed a couple of candles that were on the bed, a present meant for Miss Emily on her birthday, but by the time she returned, it was too late.

Tardy and Marion stood in silence with both their hands clasped together as they tearfully watched the nuns whispering soft prayers over Henry's body.

"Through this holy anointing, may the Lord in his love and mercy help you with the grace of the Holy Spirit."

A day that was supposed to be filled with joy and celebration, had turned into a day of mourning.

Henry had known of his heart troubles before and had stepped down from his stressful job to take it easier, but he could not have anticipated the tragic events that day.

Immediately, the bad news spread through the town like wildfire. Henry had served in the St. Thomas – St. John Municipal Council for two terms and was very popular and well-liked on the island. He also owned the Chevrolet dealership, Community Motors.

As Peggy continued walking down the street, nobody stopped to tell her the news. It wasn't until she arrived home that Adelaide, one of the housekeepers, came running down the front steps yelling.

"Mistress Creque, Mistress Creque, your husband done dead!"

Peggy never forgot those moments. She remembered every minute of that sad day so clearly as if it happened yesterday. Since then, it has been very painful for the few remaining family members, who were there, to talk about the events of that day or the loss of *Francis Bay*.

Impressions

Poems from A Small Island
© Valerie Creque-Mawson

I wrote my name upon the sand
One evening by the shore;
The sea came up upon the land
And lo! It was no more.

And though the letters that I made
Were washed from off the land,
The imprint of the outline stayed
Engraved upon the sand.

And so, death comes, and we are gone,
But still, we leave behind,
Impressions that live on and on,
Upon the sands of time.

Chapter 10

Vacationing in Cruz Bay ~ 1955

Diane Mawson, little Alana Lee Mawson, Valerie Creque-Mawson and a friend © Mawson family

A Cruz Bay Holiday

Despite being heartbroken over the loss of Francis Bay in 1954 and the death of her brother in 1957, my grandmother, Val continued to spend many wonderful holiday vacations on St. John where she found peace and solace from her pain.

In 1955, she rented a cottage in the heart of Cruz Bay for her family, with a soothing swim just a short walk away. Her modest rental, in a bright shade of pink, was tucked behind the Evangelical Lutheran Church.

It belonged to the Sewer family and still does today. Back then, the cost of the accommodation was seventy-five dollars per month. The family enjoyed their carefree days when they meandered through town or waded at the beach. There were no paved roads, telephones, or televisions on the island. The only dusty, dirt road led from Cruz Bay to Trunk Bay.

The bulldoze driver, Mr. Richards, was credited with being *an artist* for the difficult task he had in clearing the path.

The following year, the number of registered jeeps numbered fourteen. David Penn, one of the first residents with a jeep, braved the rocky road, otherwise, residents and visitors traveled primarily by boat, on horseback, or by walking.

According to the Administrator's Annual Report for 1956, the number of vehicles on the island jumped to fifty-three Jeeps, thirty-one trucks and five station wagons for a population of approximately 800 people.

Swimming, Sunning, and Shelling

The family's secluded holiday was unbelievably quiet and beautiful. It was a natural haven for them from the bustle of their busy lives in St. Thomas.

They shopped for home-grown vegetables, including squash, broccoli, and their favorite, sweet potatoes, which were plentiful. Mr. Cory Bishop had established a truck farm in *Estate Catherinberg* and was producing 2,500 pounds of quality vegetables weekly on his fifteen-acre farm.

The girls' favorite days, though, were spent swimming, sunning and shelling. They foraged along the shoreline for skipping stones and pretty shells, and afterward, picnicked on the beach. By ten o'clock in the evening, everyone was safely tucked into bed.

A Message for the Mawson Girls

One afternoon, while relaxing at their cottage, they heard a knock at their door. Slightly alarmed, they discovered that an employee from the Administrator's office had arrived with a message.

Worried that something terrible might have happened to a family member in St. Thomas, they opened the door gingerly. Without telephones or an easy way of communicating between the islands, their anxiety got the better of them, but the messenger quickly allayed their fears with good news.

He announced that Marion and Richard Miller wanted to let them know that they had a healthy baby boy. They named him Richard Michael Miller.

What a wonderful message!

Marion was Val's niece and my mother's closest cousin with whom she played at Francis Bay.

This was fabulous news for the family!

Marion was the first of the girls to marry and start a family of her own.

Emily Creque and her first grandchild, Marion van Beverhoudt-Miller

My Mom became the baby's godmother and a few years later, it was her turn to walk down the aisle.

Marlene and Dick's Honeymoon ~ 1958

My parent's wedding, which was held at Sts. Peter and Paul Catholic School in St. Thomas, was grand and beautiful!

While planning the family affair, my father suggested they spend their honeymoon on St. John. George Simmons, the St. John Administrator, was a family friend and was invited to their wedding, along with his daughter, Beryl. When Mr. Simmons learned that they were planning to honeymoon on St. John, he offered to give them a ride over on his boat that evening after the reception.

The newlyweds rented a small, wooden cottage belonging to Helen Payne across the road from the Cruz Bay beach. It was a stone's throw from the Sewer home they rented previously.

In the master bedroom was a mahogany, four-poster bed, so high off the ground that a small set of wooden stairs was needed to climb up. The following evening, they moved to what was known as the Perkins House in *Contant Enighed.*

At the turn of the century, large tracts of Sea Island cotton once grew on this hillside, but at this time, the neighborhood was dotted with small cottages which were a convenient distance to Gallows Point and Cruz Bay.

Their holiday was heavenly!

Their days were filled with romantic walks along the bay, watching the afternoon sunsets fade away. Today, one of Helen Payne's updated cottages functions as *The Terrace* restaurant.

The Death of Mrs. Emily Creque ~ 1961

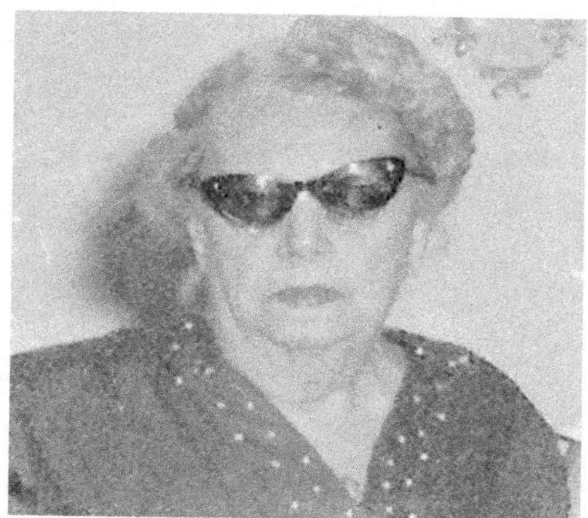

Emily Creque, 1884 – 1961 © Creque Family Archives

In 1961, Emily passed away quietly at her home in St. Thomas.

Her daughter intuitively knew that the moment was near and phoned Tardy to check up on her, reassuring herself that maybe she was mistaken.

Despite hearing that *'Miss Emily just had a cough'*, Val made the short trip from her home to be with her, fearing something far worse. While holding her mother in her arms, Emily suffered a heart attack and passed away.

It was another heartbreaking moment for Val because the two shared a special bond and were always very close. Devastated, Val turned to poetry to express her feelings about the mother she adored.

My Mother

Poems from a Small Island
Written by her daughter © Valerie Creque-Mawson

I see in your eyes that are fading
A light that is calm and clear.
And a love that is deep and eternal
For God placed His Glory there.

I see in your hair that is graying,
A halo of golden light.
A crown that the Master has promised
For doing the things that are right.

I see on your brow now furrowed
The calm sweet face of a saint
That only trials and heartaches
And suffering alone could paint.

On lips that are bravely smiling,
There trembles a breath of a prayer.
And I know that the angels are passing
And that God himself is near.

On your shoulders bent and wary,
I see there, a Holy Cross.
And your body, an earthly temple
For a soul that will never be lost.

And thus, when the Master calls you
And you answer that call from above,
You'll leave this world a better place
For the lessons of your love.

It is unfortunate indeed,
That we mistakes should make,
But let us overlook them, friend,
Forgive for God's own sake.

And when the final judgment comes
This saying will come true,
"Do unto others as you would
Have them do unto you."

A Caneel Bay Vacation ~ 1962

A year after Emily's death, my parents chose the relatively new resort of Caneel Bay for a much-needed vacation.

It had been six years since that *red-letter day* in the island's history when it became a part of the *Virgin Islands National Park.*

Since her Uncle Henry's passing and her grandmother's death, the family were no longer talking about Francis Bay.

Dick and Marlene Carney

Tea-Time Treats

My mom said, she remembered feeling completely relaxed at the hotel. Tea and cookies were served every afternoon from four to five o'clock on the covered terrace at the Turtle Bay Restaurant.

Real estate broker and businessman, Arthur Witty and his wife were vacationing at the same time. She exchanged a few pleasantries with them otherwise, their holiday was quiet and relaxing.

Garden Walks

Their days were filled with scenic garden walks, quiet reading times and refreshing swims, which lifted their spirits.

THE *Fourth* GENERATION

Valerie Creque-Mawson

Chapter 11

Finding Frank Bay ~ 1968

Frank Bay is a beautiful crescent bay located on the southwestern corner of St. John, minutes from the town of Cruz Bay. Although it's quite a distance from the Francis Bay home the family adored, it's just as captivating.

There's a reef that runs along the rocky shoreline, and along this path, a narrow passage between the rocks opens up where one can enter for a swim. It's beautiful!

A view of Frank Bay, St. John, US Virgin Islands © Valerie Sims

Nearby, are two small beachside cottages that were built during the early 1940s; rustic, charming, and full of character.

My grandmother, Val purchased the cottages in 1968 and became the fourth ancestor with ties to St. John.

Sharing a Secret

There's an interesting story about how she became aware that the owners were planning to sell them before anyone on the island knew. It had been a secret in the family for many years, until one day, she whispered it to her eldest daughter.

She told her that weeks after her son-in-law passed away, he *appeared to her in a dream* and suggested to her that she buy them. It was a dream she would never forget.

There was just one problem. The cottages weren't for sale.

Leslie, Valerie and Dick Carney © Valerie Sims

Dick's Death ~ 1968

Val's son-in-law was my mom's husband and my father, Richard Joseph Carney. He was known as Richie by his stateside family, but everyone in the islands called him Dick Carney. After a short illness, he passed away on June 20, 1968 from a blood clot that traveled from his right leg to his lungs.

It was the worst calamity that could ever have happened!

He first complained of leg pain after standing for hours waiting to see Ronald Reagan when he arrived for the Governor's conference in October 1967.

Eight months later, he was gone. Not directly from the thrombosis, he developed, but from pneumonia as well while bedridden at Knud Hansen Memorial Hospital in St. Thomas.

It's true; life changes in just a moment.

My sister Leslie and I were kids and didn't know what to say or feel.

No one in the family spoke much about feelings in those days.

The only one who did was our grandmother.

She was the intuitive one, always very spiritually connected to her family members who had passed away.

Dick Carney leaving the Cruz Bay Dock in 1967.

She adored them and spoke of them as if they were still with her. Some of her best poems were about the loved ones she lost early in her life.

The Dream ~ 1968

In the dream, my father said,

"Val, the Johansen's property is going to be up for sale.
Why don't you buy it?"

It was a strange encounter to have so soon after a loved one passed away. It was more like a conversation between two people. Nevertheless, to my grandmother, it was very real. She had several vivid experiences before where important messages were communicated to her while she slept.

She once solved a land issue for a friend when she couldn't locate a deed her husband put away just weeks before he died. Amazingly, the answer came to her in a dream when her friend's husband told her in exactly which drawer he kept the document.

Purchasing the Property

Curious to learn more, she phoned her friend Edy Johansen, one of the property owners. Edy acknowledged that her family members were thinking about selling the two cottages, but asked her how she knew, because they hadn't told anyone as yet. Not elaborating further, my grandmother simply inquired about the price they were thinking of asking. She wasn't planning on purchasing any more property but was intrigued given the unusual circumstances.

Ellen and Edith Johansen's cottages had a beautiful view that stretched beyond Great Saint James Island, with St. Thomas on the far horizon. The sunsets were breathtaking from this location.

Following through on her intuition, my grandmother purchased the property, paying $50,000 for the parcel. She signed the deed exactly six months to the day of my father's funeral, on December 23, 1968.

Selling Insurance on St. John

At the time of his death, my Dad was employed by the *Bradley and Francois Insurance Agency* in St. Thomas as an Insurance Agent.

He traveled often to St. John to visit his clients.

My sister and I also tagged along, with our nanny Veronica Gordon, spending time at the beach as he made his rounds.

Surprisingly—and as an insurance agent especially—when my Dad died, he had no life insurance for himself or his family.

The Bradley and Francois Insurance office, 1967

This was a painful disappointment for my mother, who now had two children to care for on a school nurse's salary.

The Vacation Rentals

Shortly after the cottages were purchased, my grandmother had them remodeled. My sister and I have many wonderful memories of our summer vacations at Frank Bay, swimming, sunning, and searching for uniquely-shaped rocks with our mother.

In 1971, my grandmother listed the homes on the rental market with *Holiday Homes, Inc.* A tenant moved into one of the units for $330 per month, and since then, they have been rented continually for almost fifty years.

Leslie Carney on Cruz Bay beach, 1967.

Helping the Family

When my grandmother passed away in 2002, she bequeathed the cottages to her children. The funds generated not only helped them, but one day will benefit her four grandchildren and their families which includes my first cousins, Mark and Steve, my sister and myself.

Could it be that my father's message to my grandmother was his way of helping, not only his immediate and extended family but three generations—maybe more?

As Mark Twain says, '*Truth is sometimes stranger than fiction.*

THE *Fifth* GENERATION

Marlene

Chapter 12

Moving to Contant Enighed ~ 1979

Joan, Marion & Jackie Rose van Beverhoudt, Valerie, Marlene, Diane, Shirley and Lorraine Mawson at Cassi Hill, Estate Tutu, St. Thomas © Creque Family Archives

On the Crest of Cassi Hill

Cassi Hill, on the eastern end of St. Thomas was once rolling green pastures used for grazing cattle.

As families began to move eastward from Charlotte Amalie during the 1940s, the area known as *Estate Tutu* was slowly transformed into residential parcels. My grandparents purchased five acres at the crest of Cassi Hill and built a home to raise their young family.

In the 1970s, they gave each of their daughters a plot of land nearby to build their own homes. My mother built a beautiful, Spanish-styled house with stucco walls and dark wooden beams. It was on a secluded knoll with an incredible, panoramic view of the ocean.

Every afternoon as she sat on the balcony, she admired the island of St. John in the distance. It seemed to beckon to her. Pristine and mountainous, it looked like paradise waiting to be explored. During the years she lived on Cassi Hill, more and more families moved to the surrounding valleys around her.

Because of her remote location, being only one of a handful of homes on the hill, she was targeted many times by home invaders, even after adopting a dog and installing iron-metal bars on the windows and doors.

One day, my mother decided that enough was enough. She would follow her intuition and move the family to St. John, becoming the fifth ancestor with ties to the island.

The Homesteading Act ~ 1942

Fortunately, her mother had given her a plot of land on St. John that her husband had purchased when the *Virgin Islands Homesteading Act* was initiated, and parcels were sold at a nominal cost.

Thousands of residents signed up to receive the option of securing one or more of these plots. By 1945, twenty-four homesteaders had received occupancy to their land at *Estates Contant and Enighed.*

In May 1947, my grandfather, Leon purchased six lots, 5,000 square feet each and paid approximately $319 for each of the parcels.

He was devoted to his family and exceedingly generous to them and his Catholic Church. He gave the parcels to his wife, and years later, she gave them to their daughters.

On one of these plots, my mom decided to build her dream home.

Star Villa Vacation Homes ~ 1979

My mother's husband, Chuck Selby, wanted to design a unique home that could be rented out to vacation visitors while they occupied the apartment below.

Marlene's new Star Villa Vacation home under construction in Contant Enighed.

This would build a sustainable business for her so that she could leave the job she currently held and spend more time doing what she loved; traveling, reading, and spending time with her family.

My mom was a school nurse at both Charlotte Amalie High School and later Eudora Kean High School in St. Thomas for many years.

In 1979, they designed the new home together with a unique barrel-vaulted roof made with gunite and began construction.

Star Villa Vacation Homes was one of the early entries into the vacation home rental business as we know it today. With the home completed and the business started, Chuck turned his attention to his favorite passion, flying.

Chapter 13

Casting Off over Calabash Boom 1982

Chuck Selby launching his glider over Calabash Boom © Leslie Carney

Chuck Selby had a yearning to fly! Like *Jonathan Livingston Seagull*, he felt that flying was *'power, joy, and pure beauty.'*

He launched his hang-glider 200 feet over the jagged cliffs above Calabash Boom to experience true freedom. We all thought this was a crazy thing to do, but Chuck was passionate about this sport.

Jonathan Livingston Seagull

In the mid-1970s, Chuck gave my sister and me a phenomenal little book called, *Jonathan Livingston Seagull,* by Richard Bach. Within months, it became an international bestseller, with millions of copies sold worldwide.

The story was about a seagull named Jonathan Livingston, who broke from his flock in search of freedom by pushing the bounds of conformity. This little book of wisdom was filled with many important life lessons for two, impressionable young girls. Coincidentally, Chuck's life mirrored those same messages of love, the pursuit of passion, and the importance of following your dreams that the book endorsed.

Chuck Selby

Chuck Selby was born in Detroit, Michigan in the 1930s. After serving in the Navy, marrying and having three children, Mike, Scott, and Susie, he settled in the West Indies during the latter part of his life.

When my mother met him, he had recently moved from St. Maarten to St. Thomas to start bidding on jobs to build swimming pools after his divorce. In 1980, they were married and built their home on St. John together.

Between 1979 and 1980, Chuck became fascinated with the sport of hang-gliding and wanted to be one of the first pioneers to bring the air sport to the Virgin Islands.

He enrolled in flight school at Kitty Hawk Kites' Training Center in North Carolina and flew 70 flights with a trainer.

By the time he returned to St. John, he was eager to soar over the scenic, island chain that beckoned him. He purchased a plot of land in *Calabash Boom* to build a ramp from which to jump.

His hang-glider, a Raven 209, was a lightweight glider that could be easily assembled. It was made of aluminum with large, flexible, fabric wings that made it look like a huge, colorful bird. Once he was strapped into the frame, he could control its direction by simply shifting his body weight slightly in the opposite direction.

Chuck's First Flight ~ 1982

Chuck's first launch on St. John was on September 29, 1982, a beautiful, sunny day.

He and four friends, Tuck Meachum, owner of Shipwreck restaurant, Joe Brennan of V.I. Engineering and Surveying, Scott Suit and Jack Walters—a manager at Sapphire Beach Resort—set out to conquer the thermal updrafts rising above the bay at John's Folly.

Marlene, Joe Brennan, Chuck Selby, a friend, Leslie Carney and Alana Mawson © Family Archives

Hang-Gliding Over the Hilltops

As Chuck prepared to launch first, he hooked into the glider and strapped on his bright, orange helmet.

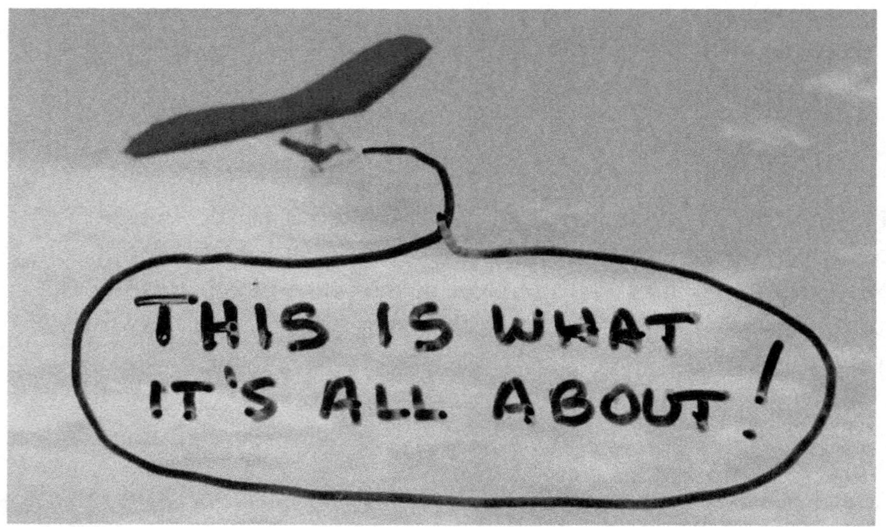

Chuck Selby © Leslie Carney

He placed his upper arms inside the uprights, lifting the glider's nose high and ran aggressively for the edge of the cliff until there was nothing below his feet but pure air.

My mom, who often tagged along on his escapades, held her breath for what seemed like an eternity.

"Why, Chuck, why?", she implored, *"Why can't you leave flying to the birds?"*

As Chuck flew down over the steep hillside below and out over the calm tranquil sea, he smiled triumphantly. Like Jonathan Seagull, he had conquered his fears. "*No more earthly worries; he was free. The only true law is that which leads to freedom. There is no other."* (Richard Bach).

Chuck glided over the tiny sailboats that looked like tiny specks of lint against his blue jeans. *So high in the sky, he was, that he could see for 1,000 miles!* He remembered, "*The gull sees farthest who flies highest."* (Richard Bach).

'As he circled above, riding the thermal to its destination, his heart raced with excitement. He could feel that he was gliding effortlessly toward a world of complete perfection'. In the air, he had the freedom to be himself, his authentic self'... all for a minute and nine-seconds'.

Flying over Costa Rica

Chuck's love of flying took him to many exotic places. While vacationing in Costa Rica in May 1987, he set out with two new friends, Arturo and Fernando, to fly above the Escazú Mountain range, not far from San José, the capital city.

Something went wrong that day. The wind may have been gusty or higher than the recommended twenty-mile-per-hour safety zone. We never knew.

All we do know is that our lives changed irreparably that day. Chuck's two friends landed safely, and he did not.

"As careful as he was, working at the very peak of his ability, he lost control." (Richard Bach)

The Road to Recovery

It took many months for Chuck to recover from this accident. Learning to walk, talk and simply write his name were difficult obstacles for him to overcome. Unbelievably, one of the first things he spoke about, was his desire to fly again.

Could it be that the joy he found in flying was so liberating that he would risk his life for it once more?

A photograph of Scott Suit © Chuck Selby

Chuck flew numerous times over *John's Folly* and *Bordeaux Mountain,* but his last flight was on that fateful day in May.

After perusing *Jonathan Livingston Seagull* again, I understood that there was nothing anyone could have done to stop Chuck from pursuing his passion for freedom and flight.

He believed, like Jonathan Gull, that we must spread our wings and reach for our dreams, wherever they take us.

"We have a reason to live!
It's to learn, to discover, to be free!"

~ Jonathan Seagull

Star Villa Vacation Homes

After the hang-gliding accident, Chuck moved back to Costa Rica for personal reasons while my mom continued to operate Star Villas on her own with a small staff.

One day, she met someone special and remarried in 2000 with a festive ceremony at Gallows Point.

Her new husband was Bob Malacarne, a teacher and active participant in *St. John Rescue, Inc.*, an organization that helps to save lives.

He was one of the first to join the group and has been an active, volunteer member since 1999.

Today, my mother is still operating *Star Villa Vacation Homes*, forty years later.

She's never worked harder in her life but has no regrets.

Bob Malacarne © Valerie Sims

She has designed the life of her dreams.

She walks every day though Cruz Bay for exercise, reads her favorite books, visits with family, and with Bob's help, takes special care of their guests and the family's properties.

THE *Sixth* GENERATION

Valerie

Chapter 14

Remembering Caneel Bay 1983

Caneel Bay Resort holds a very special place in my heart.

After college graduation, I returned to St. John to accept my first position in the "real world", becoming a *Front Desk Receptionist* at the hotel.

I loved the hospitality industry and thought this was the perfect opportunity for me to launch my career. It certainly was exciting after years of studying for a degree.

A view of Caneel Bay © Ronald R. Walker

One of my first responsibilities was greeting and welcoming new guests when they arrived at the dock. I lead them up to the breezeway for a short orientation about the hotel and its amenities, before taking them to their rooms.

Vacationing Celebrities

On one occasion, while driving guests around, the actor Mel Brooks jumped on the bus. I'll never forget his first words to me. With exuberance and a huge smile, he asked, *"did you see my latest movie?"* Without a theatre on the island, my obvious answer was, *"No, I'm sorry, I haven't."* *"You have to see it,"* he said, *"it's fabulous!"*

The movie was, *To Be or Not to Be,* with his wife, Anne Bancroft, who was also staying at the hotel. He and the actor, Alan Alda, vacationed every Christmas and stayed at Scott Beach.

There were lots of celebrities that visited the resort, and the employees were very respectful and considerate about their privacy. I quietly admired Priscilla Presley when I saw her standing near the front desk one day. She was beautiful and more petite in person than I imagined.

Diane Mawson-Walker at Caneel Bay © Ronald R. Walker

The English singer, Roger Plant from the rock band, *Led Zeppelin,* once approached me for assistance. I didn't recognize him at first, he went by the name of Mr. Green. The atmosphere at Caneel Bay was very relaxed, and you never knew who you might meet.

A Warm Welcome

I was happy when the employees warmly welcomed me, and before too long, I felt like a part of their family.

Roma, the Head Cashier, was celebrating her thirtieth year at the hotel and received a commemorative plaque and award for her service. Everyone was very excited for her.

The Front Desk Manager was Dave Larsen with Jimmy Dalmida, Sherman Callwood, and Holly Manneck as Assistant Managers.

I loved to pop around the corner to say hello to Joan Chapman, who was at the activities desk with Laurinda Connor or Deborah Ferry. They were always friendly and engaging and had fun news to share.

The bellmen, Curtis, John, Paul, and Calvin had all been there for many years before I arrived. They nodded and acknowledged me whenever they pushed the luggage cart past the Front Desk.

The Chef, John Farnsworth, was busy in the kitchen as everyone admired his beautiful sailboat anchored in the harbor.

The waiters, Denzel Clyne, and Vernon Dawson were very experienced including, Ambrose Gumbs, Noel Green, and Vernon Parsons. They knew the guests by name since the majority were repeat visitors.

Jo Sterling was the Gift Shop manager, although it was Raphie, one of the sales ladies, who I saw when an errand took me to the store.

Yolanda, who is still a close friend, made all the staff uniforms including mine, which was a wrap-around skirt in a light beige print.

Eleanor Gibney was responsible for the beautiful gardens and tropical pathways that I followed on my errands. I loved the subtle way they were lit at night.

Captain Edwin Sullivan and his deckhand, Peter, always greeted me with warm smiles, even thirty years later when I spotted Captain Sullivan on the ferry and shared a heartwarming embrace. He was happy to see me and pose for this selfie photo in 2013.

The author with Captain Sullivan

One endearing employee I'll never forget was Cornelius Matthias. He was the proud Captain of the *Lady Cornelius,* a 22-foot Pearson Ensign, first built in 1962. He took guests sailing to Congo and Lovango Cay for a snorkel, never taking more than two at a time. This gave him the opportunity of engaging with them about the island's history on a more intimate level.

According to Margaret Enos, *"Cornie spun yarns with the best of them, and his stories added charm to each three-hour sail."*

Many were surprised to learn that for nearly nine years, Cornie had commuted to work on horseback, a three-hour ride from his Coral Bay home, leaving at 4:30 am on a Monday and returning on a Saturday. He was a kind gentleman; respected and revered by everyone.

There were many more employees, busy behind the scenes that I didn't have the opportunity to meet or get to know. These mentioned were just a few out of the dozens that worked together to make Caneel Bay a special place.

The Buffet at Turtle Bay

The resort hosted many wonderful functions with sumptuous buffets during my tenure, but one evening, in particular, was the most memorable for me.

It was a holiday dinner held at the Turtle Bay Restaurant for dignitaries from the British Virgin Islands. A boat full of BVI guests arrived at the dock after sunset and I was responsible for greeting them and driving everyone up to the festivities. It was the first time I wore an evening gown and high heels to work and I felt like a princess. My dress was a form-fitting strapless gown made of black velvet with a spider brooch pinned at the center. It glimmered and sparkled when it reflected the light, making me feel very special.

On the boat that evening was the Chief Minister and other officials including H. Lavity Stout, Cyril Romney, Ralph O'Neal, and a very special guest to me, Henry O. Creque, the Speaker of the Legislative Council.

Mr. Creque was the nephew of my second, great grandfather and was named after him. He was a quiet and modest gentleman who shared his knowledge and experience freely with the younger generation.

This was the first time we had ever met, and I spent the entire evening conversing with him at dinner. It was as if there was no one else in the room!

Everyone wondered what we both had in common that made the conversation so engaging. Unbeknownst to them, we shared a deep interest in family history. The details of our long discussion escape me, but the magical feeling of being on top of the world that night was unforgettable.

Cocktail Parties on the Starlight Terrace

The weekly cocktail party held on the Starlight Terrace was a festive event guests enjoyed. It was hosted by the General Manager, Michael Glennie, and was the perfect opportunity for him to greet and welcome all the new arrivals personally.

They were delighted when they saw the balcony's perimeter aglow with flickering tiki torches. It created an enchanting environment, especially on nights when the moon was full, and the stars were bright. At the top of the landing, the steel band played rhythmic melodies. After cocktails and hors d'oeuvres were served, guests began to relax and look forward to the beginning of their holiday.

The Caneel Bay Terrace © Ronald R. Walker

On my evening shift, when I heard the fun entertainment permeating through the front desk area below, it created an atmosphere that made me feel happy to be working there.

The Sunset Cruises

Another holiday highlight for many of the visitors was the daily sunset cruise. It left the dock just in time to catch the views of the setting sun before returning in time for dinner.

They were very popular, and when booked to capacity, I was asked to assist the deckhand, which was exciting for me.

As the boat slowly drifted away from the dock, I offered the passengers a tray of delicacies, including fried shrimp and a variety of sweet and tangy dipping sauces to accompany them.

Once out of the bay, cocktails were served, and everyone chatted and introduced themselves to each other, making new friends as the journey began.

The Caneel Bay ferry © Ronald R. Walker

Since we traveled at a slow cruising speed, it allowed the passengers to walk around, catching a last glimpse of the hotel before we motored to Honeymoon Beach.

When they glanced back at the bay, they could see the faint outline of vacationers as they soaked up the last rays of the setting sun.

Bathing the horizon were the brightest hues of apricot, coral, and tangerine. The ever-changing colors were like a painter's palette that everyone admired from the distance.

A Bird-Feeding Frenzy

When the guests finished their nibbles and began to unwind, they casually discarded the shrimp tails overboard. It's the reason why a small group of noisy seabirds always trailed behind the boat during these outings. They knew they could expect an easy treat.

Known as *Terns*, they had a slender build with long, forked tails and narrow wings. Sometimes, they followed the boat so closely, I felt I could reach out and touch them.

Just before the shrimp tails hit the water, the birds swooped down, plunging and darting to snatch them in mid-flight, squawking at each other loudly.

We watched with amazement as they fought and competed for the tasty prizes before they sank below the surface. Their accuracy was incredible!

Terns ~ Scavengers of the water © flickr.com

These birds, with their sharp, hooked bills, were known as *nature's scavengers of the water.*

During my tenure at Caneel Bay, there were many times I felt more like a guest than an employee.

I didn't receive any special consideration but was simply happy to be working in a beautiful tropical setting.

Scuba Diving Adventures

Jim Travers, the charismatic Dive Master, was larger than life! He and first mate, Bob Shinners introduced guests to the exciting adventures of scuba diving, including night dives, and wreck diving. Jim had a presence about him that made one believe he owned the establishment, and in many ways, he did. In his Speedo bikini, he waltzed by the front desk every day, greeting the attendants with, *Hello, Babydoll*, a term of endearment popularized in the 1950s.

No one seemed to mind. On the contrary, his confidence and southern charm always made them chuckle. Jim regularly shared the most outlandish and unbelievable stories, entertaining everyone within listening distance. Although his escapades were incredible at times, he brought huge smiles and laughter to those around him.

One endearing trait that Jim possessed, more than others, was his generosity. He helped everyone with everything. If someone needed air tanks filled or to borrow equipment or even tag along on his boating excursions for free, Jim said yes. He took care of everybody.

He was exceedingly generous and often gave away lobster or fresh fish that he caught every time his boat returned with a full catch. All the employees loved him for that.

Looking for Lobsters

Jim taught me how to scuba dive and pretty soon, I was fishing and hunting for lobsters too.

What an exhilarating experience, swimming over the reefs, sixty-five feet below the surface, scanning the rocks for protruding antennae! Every one of my senses was fixated on the rocks and ledges around me, anxious to catch the first glimpse of something moving.

When I did spot a lobster, I approached and gently placed my snare over the extended antennae, moving it gingerly down to the knuckle. As I pulled sideways with a quick snap of the wrist, the snare closed, and I could feel my heart pounding through my chest as I pulled the crustacean out of his protective hole.

Jim Travers, the Scuba Instructor at Caneel Bay Resort © Valerie Carney

Face to face with my wiggling catch, I could hear my breathing as it became louder and faster through the regulator, magnifying the exhilarating feeling of excitement and discovery.

Snaring lobsters was fun but bagging them was not. I was always afraid I would lose my prize. Luckily, Godwin Callwood came to my rescue on many occasions when the lobsters frantically flapped their tails in a last-ditch effort to escape.

Gizmo, as Godwin was affectionately known, was born in Jost van Dyke, and worked for Jim for many years. Not only did he fill the tanks and maintain the dive boat, but he was also Jim's closest friend and right-hand man.

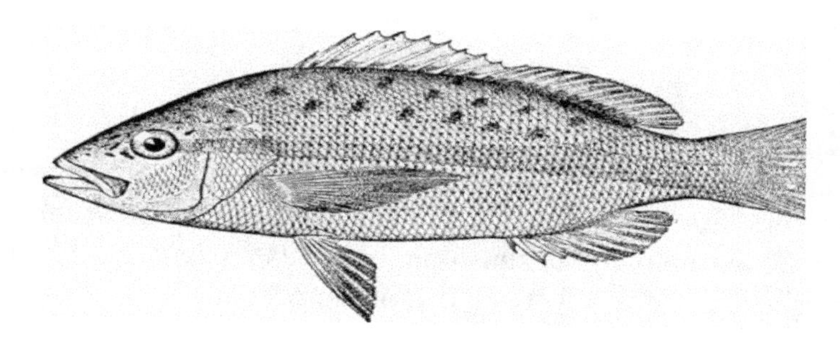

Bottom Fishing

Soon, we were fishing late at night and bringing bins of fresh yellowtail snappers to supply all the restaurants.

Gizmo was the best fisherman I've ever met! He could bring up two snappers on his line at the same time, hand-over-hand, and fill his thirty-gallon bin before anyone else on the boat! Whatever fish were left, would be sold in Cruz Bay, or more likely, given away. Jim was generous to a fault. It's probably what made him a celebrity in a small town.

Fish Fries

A few of Jim's closest friends had the opportunity of enjoying the snappers freshly prepared for them.

After filleting several, he seasoned them lightly with breadcrumbs, then pan-fried them with Danish butter until fully cooked. He then prepared his special, homemade cocktail sauce to accompany them.

It was a mixture of horseradish, ketchup, Worcestershire, hot pepper sauce, with a dash of salt and pepper, topped with the juice of a freshly squeezed lime. His friends were amazed at how tasty and delicious fresh fish could be!

Docking the Jumbie Jay

There came a time when I felt a bit stifled behind the front desk and went to work for Jim, operating the snorkel tours. It gave me the chance to be outdoors in the sunshine, but it also meant that I had to learn to drive and dock a forty-five-foot motorboat.

On one unforgettable day, Jim gave me the wheel of the *Jumbie Jay*, with a few hasty instructions on how to dock the vessel and sent me into the middle of the harbor. Fortunately, Gizmo was standing at the stern.

"Bring the vessel alongside, and whatever you do, don't crash into the dock!" he yelled. This was my very first attempt to dock a boat!

When Jim let the bow and stern lines go, I hesitantly headed out toward the channel, panicking inside at this request. I didn't want to disappoint him or damage the boat.

When I got to the middle of the bay, I slowly turned the wheel and began my first approach. My heart was pulsing as my hands tightly gripped the wheel. I must have made at least ten attempts and couldn't swing the boat around fast enough so that the stern faced the beach.

I wanted to give up, but that was not an option. Jim refused to let me quit!

He sent me out again and again to the middle of the bay to turn around and approach once more.

I was near tears and embarrassed as everyone on the beach stopped to watch my struggles and failures. I never scraped the boat, but I couldn't bring it in alongside the dock.

Finally, a feeling of confidence kicked in on my last approach, and I gunned the engines as I made my turn. This action swung the stern closer to the dock and the *Jumbie Jay* pulled alongside beautifully. As everyone clapped, I finally let the tears flow.

Since that day, I've never forgotten how to dock a vessel! I went on to get my fifty-ton ocean operator's license, which came in handy ten years later when my husband and I opened Billy Bones Beach Bar and Grill on Norman Island. I drove the staff over every day in our thirty-foot Island Hopper, before a permanent captain could be found.

A Majestic Manta Ray

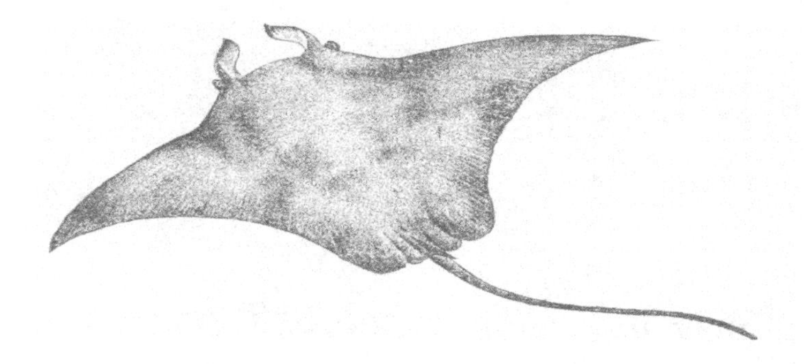

Feeling confident behind the wheel, I began taking Caneel guests on snorkel tours to nearby islands on the *Jumbie Jr.*, a smaller boat. It was a rustic, native craft, originally called, *All Ah We,* transformed to add a small ramp for the snorkeling excursions.

After teaching the snorkeling lessons on the beach every day, the guests were eager to sign up for the tours. Henley Cay and Congo Cay were two of their favorite stops.

On one occasion, while snorkeling off of Henley Cay with my group, a giant Manta ray swam uncomfortably close. Time seemed to stand still as we watched him gracefully coasting through the shallows with his huge expansive wings, turning left and then right. He glided effortlessly through the water, seemingly unaware of us.

My eyes followed his every move in disbelief. I had never been so close to something so huge! I felt responsible for the guests should anything happen, but they were delighted and weren't afraid. This experience turned out to be the highlight of their visit!

In the olden days, Manta rays were called, *Devilfish*. Their horn-shaped fins gave them an evil appearance, and many were hunted out of curiosity.

Being in the presence of this majestic giant reminded me how very small and insignificant I was. With his immense size and aura, I was quickly reminded that I was only a visitor in his undersea world.

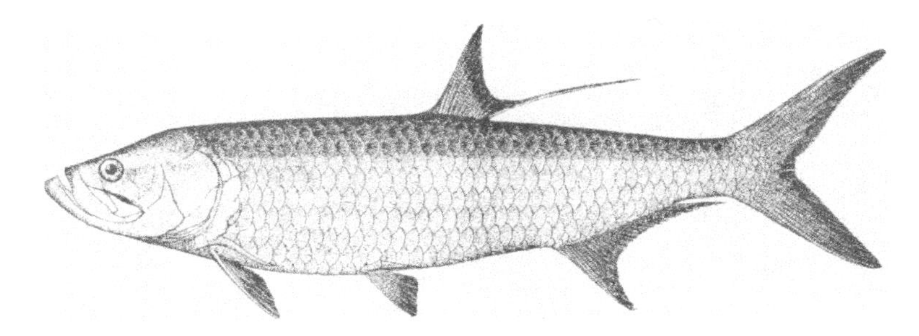

Swimming with Schools of Tarpon

Swimming among large schools of Tarpon, on the other hand, was especially intimidating to me. I didn't see them often, but when we encountered them near Congo Cay one day, I held my breath for what seemed like an eternity.

There must have been about 100 of them, all staring at me!

These air-breathing fish with huge eyes and broad mouths were much larger and scarier than the lone barracuda we often encountered. Being in deeper water and farther from our home base added to my anxiety.

Tarpons are prized not only because of their great size, but also because of the fight they put up and their incredible leaping ability. Tarpon tournaments are popular and there are numerous competitions held around the world.

I loved being outdoors and showing the guests the colorful fish, and exotic wildlife the islands offered. Once I warmed up after the morning snorkel tour, the most difficult part of the job was getting into the *cold water* for the afternoon trip.

During my short tenure at Caneel Bay, I learned to appreciate the island's beauty, both above and below the surface. Fishing, scuba diving, and operating a motor vessel are valuable skills that I was never taught at college. I'm grateful I had the opportunity to learn them in such an enchanted environment.

Returning for a Visit ~ July 2017

For the first time in many years, I returned in the summer of 2017 to visit Caneel Bay and any employees still working at the hotel.

I expected to see lots of familiar faces, as if I had never left, but was dismayed when everywhere I turned, I didn't find anyone I knew. Of course, it had been a long time since I had worked there, but Caneel employees tended to stay a lifetime.

I asked the front desk personnel to be sure. *Do you recognize me? Do I look familiar to you?* Each one shook their heads. I went to the bellman's station—much larger in structure than I remembered—and found one bellman. *Do you know me?* He shook his head, no.

I had somehow expected everything to be as I remembered as if nothing had changed, like returning home after an extended trip abroad. Disillusioned at not having found anyone I could reconnect with, I paused to take a few photographs of the beautiful beach I remembered so well.

The Caneel Bay beach © 2017 Valerie Sims

Hurricanes Irma and Maria ~ 2017

Two months after my visit, on September 6, Hurricane Irma hit the Virgin Islands and on September 19, Hurricane Maria made landfall, one of the worst natural disasters in recorded history to affect the islands.

Never could I have imagined that not only did everyone I had known disappear, but the very buildings I had once worked in were gone! Caneel Bay was no more, and all my experiences were now only faded memories. Immediately, I knew how Henry and my grandmother must have felt when they discovered that the Francis Bay home had been sold and was gone forever. It was like a death in the family.

It's heart-wrenching to realize that nothing will ever be the same again. Only time will tell what becomes of the beautiful property once known as *Caneel Bay Resort*.

THE *Seventh* GENERATION

Chapter 15

The Seventh Generation

The author's children at the Annaberg ruins on St. John © Valerie Sims

My husband and I have two children who love St. John too. They don't live on the island full-time, but they've enjoyed summer holidays and special times with their grandparents at Star Villas. When my nephews were young, they too spent their summers hiking the island and swimming at Frank Bay in the afternoons.

Recently, I asked our teenage daughter what she loved most about St. John and she summed it up perfectly in one sentence.
She said, *"I love the sound of nature."*

The opportunity to feel connected to nature on a deeper level is what St. John has represented for generations to our family. The natural beauty found on the island connects us all to something greater than ourselves. Our children are too young to have enjoyed a lifetime of memories, but perhaps one day, they'll accumulate a few stories of their own to share with their descendants.

Summary

We've come to the end of a journey through seven generations of St. John's incredible history!

I hope you've enjoyed learning a little more about the island's past through our family's experiences. These shared memories are just a small fragment of the tapestry to which thousands have contributed to over the years.

Fresh fish arrives for everyone. © The Royal Library of Denmark

A Close-Knit Community

Without a strong survival ethic, the island's close-knit community would never have overcome the insurmountable hurdles tossed into their path. St. Johnians have an indelible spirit that can't be tamed and after every setback, they came back… *stronger*.

Being miles from the nearest sizable settlement, compelled neighboring families to work together by hunting, fishing, and farming. It was the secret to their survival.

Property owners contributed too by turning their estates into commercial enterprises. This helped laborers earn a living. Unfortunately, there were many obstacles to overcome with the unpredictable weather. Both the dry season and the hurricane season had disastrous effects on the crops.

The Church pastors were invaluable as well and nurtured a sense of unity and togetherness within the community. Their comforting nature was important when hard times hit.

Laurance Rockefeller

There's no question Laurance Rockefeller and his associates played a major role in shaping the island's conservation values as we know them today. Some may be curious about the amounts received and exactly what was said to the landowners who donated their lands or to those who sold their properties, but the fact that St. John has maintained its intrinsic beauty for all to enjoy, is a wonderment.

A Promise Made ~ 1956

When the *Virgin Islands National Park* was established, the Secretary of the Interior promised that the government would take *good care* of St. John's verdant hills and valleys.

"The value of these lands," he said, *"cannot be featured in monetary terms, for their true value lies in the countless hours of wholesome enjoyment, spiritual refreshment and mental solace that they bring."*

Harmony through Healing

Interestingly, no promises were ever made regarding the ancestral people of the island and their needs. Rockefeller and the Department of the Interior's main interest was always about preserving the land and the environment, not the culture of the people.

St. Johnians will have to take care of themselves as they have done for centuries.

While they live on an island in which the wildlife, natural beauty, and historical sites are preserved for the enjoyment of all, it's imperative that *their ancestral stories* and *rich heritage* be safeguarded as well.

St. Johnians - 1930s © Valerie Sims, Creque Family Archives

Documenting them from their living descendants and creating a space for them in the community should be a priority, sentiments the *St. Jan Heritage Collective* recently shared.

Only then will harmony prevail, when the preservation of their narratives becomes just as important as the preservation of their former lands.

A Love for the Land

This journey, one that began with an investment by a distant relative, has given me a new appreciation for those who lived during these tumultuous times, and I hope it does for you too.

Eugène's love for the land has extended through seven generations of his descendants.

Although it cost him his life, it created an opportunity for his progeny to appreciate the island's beauty for themselves and find their own spiritual connections. Indeed, they did and discovered an unbreakable bond with an island so many people love.

The Last Descendant

Despite the heartbreak Emily's children experienced when they discovered that the Francis Bay home was gone forever, a few of the siblings continued to spend time on the island, making new memories.

Today, only one of Eugène's direct descendants calls the island home and appreciates the beauty her ancestor first discovered.

The little girl, who was always so seasick on the boat, is the last to carry the torch, representing more than one hundred and twenty years of love for the little island of *St. John*.

Diane and Marlene gaze at the ruins of the Francis Bay home they love. © Ronald R. Walker

The End

Reverie

Poems from A Small Island

When the cows are in the barnyard
And the chickens in their coops
And the evening hour is falling soft and gray.

When the birds have ceased their twitter
And the golden sun has set
And we realize that it's the close of day.

Then we gather 'round the old folks
In that dear old-fashioned home
And they tell us tales of spirits, legends long.

And when our eyes grow sleepy
And it's time to go to bed
Grandma always sings us an old-fashioned song.

Fragrant jasmines from the garden
Round the window start to creep
Just as they did in days so long gone by.

And we dream the tales they tell us
Happy, peaceful, childhood sleep
While the night wind softly croons a lullaby.

The moon looks down in splendor
On the glistening beach so white
Where the sea throws up the shells and seaweed green
And I wonder what those folks are doing far away tonight.
God, send your blessing on that peaceful scene.

The old folks have all vanished
They have died there one by one
While the old home looks out at the sea alone.
God, bless that truthful poet, who once said these simple words,
"There is no place on earth, like Home Sweet Home!"

Notes

St. John Lands the Creque Family Once Owned

Clockwise: Henry, Frank, Emily, Olga Val, and little Margie Creque © Creque Family Archives

Lime Tree Bay, 1920

Herman's first purchase on St. John was *5G Lime Tree Bay*, otherwise known as *Haulover Bay*. On August 14, 1920, he bought eight acres from Oswald George for $500.

Later, in January 1945, it became part of a *Deed of Gift* from Herman to his property manager, Fritz Allan Smith. Herman was always thoughtful and very generous, giving freely of his time, his money and his lands. The deed read:

"For and in consideration of the faithful service of Fritz Allan Smith of St. John and one dollar paid by him, I do hereby give my Estate Lime Tree Bay, known as 5G Haulover, East End Quarter to him. I, Emily, wife of Herman, join my husband in the above deed and wave all my rights of dower and other rights to the premises."

Estate Lamesure ~ 1922

Herman purchased Great and Little Lamesure, Estate Hope, Misgunst, Parforce, Cabritte Horn, Bakkero and Concordia on May 8, 1922, from Lieutenant Seth Lagerstadt, assuming his mortgage of $13,500. The total price paid was $15,000 for all the estates. Later, in May 1953, his widow, Emily sold these estates to David Stick who was representing his father, Frank Stick and his investors. In 1956, they formed part of the new, Virgin Islands National Park.

5A Bordeaux ~ 1922

This property was purchased on May 8, 1922 from Seth Lagerstadt. In March of 1951, Emily gave the Municipality of St. John a parcel of this land measuring 5,439 square feet as a gift. A cistern may have been built on the property, hence the government's interest.

5F Bordeaux ~ 1924

On April 30, 1924, Herman purchased four acres of *5F Bordeaux* from Mr. Jorgensen before he left the island, paying $100 for the land. Lawyer J.P. Jorgensen owned many estates on both St. Thomas and St. John.

He was familiarly called, *'the old lawyer',* not because he was old, but because *'he looked older than he was, especially when he forgot to have his flowing locks clipped.'*

Otherwise, he was young and vigorous in both mind and body and possessed a good sense of wit and humor. *'He knew everybody and everything,'* it was said.

In 1924, Mr. Jorgensen returned to Denmark and settled in Horsens where his wife had been buried six years earlier.

JP Jorgensen © The Royal Library of Denmark

This property later formed part of a May 1953 sale to David Stick/Frank Stick and later became a part of the *Virgin Islands National Park.*

13AA Friis Bay ~ 1927

Estate Friis Bay was purchased from Gustave and Rosita Bornn on June 11, 1927. It was included in the adjudication of the Estate of Herman O. Creque as belonging to him at the time of his death, however, further research turned up a deed in which Herman gave this land to his overseer, Fritz Allan Smith in January of 1945.

Herman was very grateful to Fritz and gifted him close to one hundred acres of his St. John lands.

The view of the beach at Estate Friis Bay © Valerie Sims

The total acreage for this estate was 73 acres. Today, his descendants operate Miss Lucy's Restaurant on this property.

Estate Mary's Point/Francis Bay ~ 1927

Estate Mary's Point was purchased on June 27, 1927 from Mrs. Estella Stakemann for $6,500.00. The 250-acre estate formed part of the sale to Jackson Hole Preserve, Inc. on December 30, 1954, along with the estates of Annaberg and Concordia.

14G and 14H Johns Folly ~ 1927

Herman purchased two acres, known as *14H Johns Folly* from Gustave Bornn. He also purchased six acres, known as *14G Johns Folly*. In 1947, he gifted these parcels to Fritz Allan Smith as well, for his *'faithful service.'*

Estate Concordia ~ 1930

After J.P. Jorgensen died in January of 1926, his remaining property on St. John was put up for public auction. Herman purchased *15B Estate Concordia* from the *Estate of J.P. Jorgensen.* (Probate No. 4/1926). He paid $315 for 200 acres on March 26, 1930. The property later formed part of a deed to Jackson Hole Preserve, Inc. on December 30, 1954, along with *Mary's Point* and *Annaberg Estate.*

4-O Maho Bay Quarter ~ 1932

Herman purchased one acre of land from Herbert E. Lockhart, near Francis Bay on March 17, 1932.

Estate Annaberg ~ 1932 and 1935

In 1932, Herman purchased 197 acres of Annaberg for $2,250 from Carl Francis. In 1935, he bought the balance of the estate, fifty acres from Herbert E. Lockhart for $900.00. This gave him ownership of the entire estate, 247 acres. These lands and others were included in the option to Frank Stick and later sold to *Jackson Hole Preserve, Inc.* on December 30, 1954.

4-U Maho Bay Quarter ~ 1935

This parcel was a beautiful, one-acre plot overlooking *Francis Bay* that Herman purchased from Arabella Blyden. She inherited it from her husband, William. It was known as the *School House lot.*

In 1925, it once belonged to Earle Francis, the son of Carl Francis. Herman purchased the acre for $100 on August 30, 1935. At one time, back in 1904, this land yielded '*a fine crop of canes and bananas*'. Both 4-0 and 4-U were later sold by Herman's heirs.

The Island of Mingo Cay ~ 1936

With a view to expanding his hunting grounds, Herman purchased the island of Mingo Cay—also known as 23 Saint Senior Island—from Alice Smith, a widow of Lovango Cay. He paid $800. The fifty-acre parcel is located in Pillsbury Sound between St. Thomas and St. John. ~ *August 10, 1936*

On January 29, 1985, Herman's heirs sold the island to Ruth Gordon McGill of Austin, Texas for $450,000. She later transferred it to a company, *Mingo Cay, LLC* in 2003.

Pottery found on Little St. James by a friend.

The Island of Little Saint James ~ 1936

In December of 1936, Herman purchased the island of *Little Saint James* from Edward George for $450. It was known as 6B Redhook Quarter and located on the southwestern side of St. John.

Mr. George enjoyed quiet and undisturbed possession of the fifty-acre island for more than twenty years but had no recorded title.

During the nineteenth century, the island was popular among hunting parties in search of wild goats. Herman too, used the location for the same purpose, finding food for his family and laborers.

QUAY
LITTLE ST. JAMES,
BETWEEN
ST. THOMAS AND ST. JOHNS,
FOR SALE.

SEALED TENDERS to be received up to
4TH OF OCTOBER,
and to be opened said day, 12 o'clock, at No. 34, 35 *a*, Queen's Street King's Quarter.

Conditions for sale to be seen at the Printing-office.

Dealing of Vice-Governor H. H. Berg, *St. Thomas, 12th September*, 1862.

H. KREBS.
CHRISTIAN HOSKLÆR.

On August 13, 1981, his heirs sold the island for $470,000 to Arch W. Cummin of New York.

On April 27, 1998, Mr. Cummin transferred the island to LSJ, LLC., Jeffrey Epstein's company, for $7,950,000. After a survey, the island was found to be 68.7 acres.

During the 1990s, Little St. James was advertised as a private retreat, "crowned with a magnificent vacation villa where coral stone walls, sweeping arches, and gothic columns framed 360-degree views of aquamarine waters."

Inside boasted of "richly decorated spacious interiors and fine European antique furnishings," including a video room with an antique sleigh bed.

From brochure photographs, it's evident that the home was surrounded by beautiful tropical gardens with views of the sea from every room.

Unfortunately, Little St. James is currently involved in one of the nation's most salacious stories. It's often referred to in the news as *Pedophile Island* or *Little St. Jeff's* because of the alleged abuse of underage girls that were brought there under false pretenses.

View from 16B Molendahl in Coral Bay © Valerie Sims, Creque Family Archives

16B Mollendahl ~ 1936

Herman purchased 16B Molendahl on the eastern side of St. John from Anna Catherine Parker on December 11, 1936.

It was located near the entrance to *Lamesure Estate* on the right-hand side of the road and overlooked the pond and harbor. He paid $8 for 2+ acres in a quitclaim deed.

By a deed dated January 4, 1989, and signed by a resident of Hard Labor, the remainder of 16B Mollendahl, which appears to have included Emily's land, was sold onto a New York developer, without the family's knowledge.

Emily's descendants were not aware of this parcel, even though it had been adjudicated to her after the 1949 death of her husband. By the time this was confirmed by a title search at the *Office of the Recorder of Deeds,* more than twenty years had passed since the property's sale.

2AA Store Caneel Bay ~ 1938

Herman purchased *2AA Store Caneel Bay* from the *Estate of J.P. Jorgensen* in June 1938. The history of what became of this parcel is still being researched and will be updated at a later date.

15A Estate Rendezvous and Ditleff ~ 1938

Estate Rendezvous and Ditliff was a very large property Herman acquired from the *Estate of J.P. Jorgensen* on February 24, 1938. It encompassed over 270 acres.

On November 18, 1946, Herman sold this estate for $6,000 to the purchaser, Clide Eugene Osborn of Live Oak, Florida.

Two years later, on July 1, 1948, Mr. Osborn died reportedly from injuries he received from a shark attack while in the water at Ditliff Bay. He was forty-six years old. Herman was devastated when he heard the sad news, having met and spoken to Clide on many occasions.

The Virgin Islands Daily News carried the horrifying details on July 6, 1948.

Man Reported Eaten by Shark in Genti Bay
July 1, 1948

'About fifty yards from shore, it was reported that Clide Osborn fell or jumped off his boat, Shadow I.

'The boatman, William George, tried to induce him to get back on board, but he refused. Soon afterward, he hollered to the boatman that he had been attacked by a shark!

'He was last seen being pulled underwater. A thorough search of the waters and the area failed to reveal any trace of the body.'

According to a report by Clide's step-brother, Frank L. Cramer:

'Young Osborne was an engineer, and at the time of the accident was in his cabin cruiser, which he purchased about a year and a half before the accident. He was preparing to build a hotel for vacationists on St. John, which he believed was the most beautiful of all the islands.

Mr. Osborne had a companion with him on the boat at the time of the accident and he reported his tragic death to the family.

.

Clide purchased land on St. John and had been working there for some time and expected to bring his family to the island as soon as accommodations could be made.

Mr. Osborne was 6-foot tall, weighed 180 pounds, and was of an athletic type. He loved the climate and scenic beauty of the islands.'

Clide had three children, a son and two daughters, with the eldest being Clide, Jr., who was twenty-two years old at the time.

In January of 2018, Clyde Jr. died at the age of 92.

Bibliography

Bach, Richard, *Jonathan Livingston Seagull*, Macmillan Publishers, 1970.

Bennett, Jacob, *The Complete Guide to Grass-fed Cattle: How to Raise Your Cattle on Natural Grass for Fun and Profit,* Atlantic Publishing Group, Inc., 2011.

Fine, John Christopher, *Lost on the Ocean Floor; Diving the World's Ghost Ships*, Annapolis, Maryland: Naval Institute Press, 2005.

Gibney, Eleanor, Knight, Sr. David, W., Schoonover, Bruce and Swan, Robin, *St. John, Life in Five Quarters*, Selected readings from the Archives of the St. John Historical Society, 2010.

Hatch, Jr., Charles E., *Reef Bay (Par Force) Estate House and Sugar Factory*, Virgin Islands National Park, Historic Structures Report, History Data, Department of the Interior, June 1969.

Hubler, Harold A., *A Report on the Proposal to Establish the Island of St. John as a National Park or Monument,* 1939.

Jakobsen, Arne Handberg, *Countess Daisy,* Published through Lulu (dot) com, 2014.

Jarvis, J. Antonio, *The Virgin Islands and Their People,* Dorrance & Company, 1944.

Kapok Chronicles, *The Establishment of Virgin Islands National Park*, National Park Service, US Depart of the Interior, Park News, Summer/Fall 2006.

Knight, Sr. David, W., *Understanding Annaberg, A Brief History of Estate Annaberg on St. John, US Virgin Islands,* Little Nordside Press, 2002.

Knight, Sr. David, W., *Cruz Bay, From Conquest to Exploitation, A Forgotten History,* 2017.

Low, Ruth Hull and Valls, Lito, *St. John Backtime: Eyewitness Accounts from 1718 to 1956,* Newtown, Ct., Eden Hill Press, 1985.

Mawson, Valerie Creque, *Poems from a Small Island,* Posterity Press, Chevy Chase, Maryland, 2009.

Near, Don, Frank Stick*: Unsung Hero of VINP's Creation?* St. John Times, August 2004.

O'Neal, Joseph Reynold, *Life Notes, Reflections of a British Virgin Islander,* U.S. Xlibris Corporation, 2004.

Rockresorts, Inc. *The Caneel Bay Welcome Booklet,* and *The Clipper Newsletter*, March 1983.

Sims, Valerie, *Henry O. Creque, A Biography 1858-1915,* Road Town, Tortola, British Virgin Islands, 2010.

Stick, Frank, *Prospectus for the Development of Estate Lameshur, St. John, Virgin Islands,* April 1953.

Stokes, Anson Phelps, *Cruising in the West Indies,* Dodd, Mead, and Co., 1902.

Taylor, Charles E., *Leaflets from the Danish West Indies,* William Dawson and Sons, London, 1888.

The New York Times, *Canoe Adventurer Talked to Sharks,* Sept 23, 1928.

The New York Times, *Lone Canoe Voyager Arrives at St. Thomas,* September 9, 1928.

Thruelsen, Richard, *The Island Nobody Spoiled,* Saturday Evening Post, 1955.

Tuxen, Jan, *The Notorious Lawyer Jorgensen of St. Thomas,* Jens Peter Jorgensen (1848-1926), 2011.

Zabriskie, Luther K. *The Virgin Islands of the United States of America,* G.P. Putnam's Sons, The Knickerbocker Press, New York, 1918.

Acknowledgements

I would like to express my sincerest gratitude to several individuals and organizations, who in one way or another, contributed to the publication of this book.

A special thank you to Marlene Malacarne, Bob Malacarne and Leslie Carney for their support and encouragement. A very heartwarming thank-you to my husband, David Sims, and our children for their untiring patience and understanding. I love you!

I'm especially grateful to those who provided the stories, photographs, digital images, and documents shared within these pages, namely:
Herman and Emily Creque, Valerie Creque-Mawson, Leon A. Mawson, Alana Lee Mawson, Charles C. Selby, Richard and Marion Miller, Esther Drum (Tootie), William (Bill) Creque, Henry O. Creque and Margaret (Peggy) Creque, Henry Owen Creque, IV, Ronald and Diane Walker, Aimee de Lagarde and her son, Kevin de Lagarde, Thelma Meyers, Elaine Thorne, Dr. Paul M. Pearson, David and Barbara Grove, Bruce and Sharon Schoonover, Francis LeCuyer, Chuck Pishko, Marian Czukoski, Pearson Scott Freeman, David W. Knight, Sr., Mary Alice Ballenger, Shirley Gilker, David Star Jordan, James Alexander Henshall, Dr. Dante Beretta, Elaine Estern, Ronald Lockhart, John Bedford Creque and Dave Horner.

Thank you to the Royal Danish Library in Copenhagen, Denmark for indexing the island's newspapers, the Maritime Museum of Denmark, the Danish Ministry of Culture, the National Archives in Washington, DC, the Archives of the British Virgin Islands, The Virgin Islands Daily News, Ancestry.com, FamilySearch.org, the Enid M. Baa Library, the Elaine Ione Sprauve Library, the Charles W. Turnbull Regional Library in the US Virgin Islands and the always helpful librarian there, Miss Beverly Smith.

I couldn't have shared these stories without all of your contributions.

About the Author

Valerie Sims

Valerie's love of family history all started with wonderful conversations with her grandmother!

Learning about her life growing up under the Danish flag inspired her fascination with genealogy and family history as a young girl.

In 2010, she captured the top prize for the *Deputy Governor's History Research Award* in the British Virgin Islands for her research paper. It was about her second great-grandfather entitled, *The Life of Henry O. Creque, 1857 to 1915, A Biography*.

Today, she researches and writes for her website, ***VintageVirginIslands.com***. It offers over 300 blog posts about the history of the US Virgin Islands, the Danish West Indies, and the British Virgin Islands.

She also has fun creating products for ***ShopViHistory.com*** to bring the islands' past alive with puzzles, notebooks, and prints. Each one has a fascinating story to tell!

Vintage St. John is her first book. She hopes it will inspire others to document their family stories and keep their heritage alive.

Valerie and her husband currently make their home in the Caribbean raising their two children with an ever-watchful eye on their two, rambunctious little dogs.

Follow Me on the Web!

If you've enjoyed this book, please send me a message. I would love to hear from you! I'm also on facebook every day, so we can connect there:

- Email address: VintageVI@icloud.com
- Follow me on facebook with 7,000+ fans at Facebook.com/VintageVirginIslands
- Pin with me on Pinterest with 20,000+ monthly viewers
- For book purchases, visit: VintageStJohnBook.com

Vintage St. John is available on amazon.com, selected retail stores in the US Virgin Islands and at the office of Star Villa Vacation Homes in *Estate Contant Enighed*, across the street from Battery Hill.

For more stories about St. John, visit VintageStJohn.com

Now that this fun project is completed, I'm working on another exciting one!

Sign up here for updates: ValerieSims.com/newsletter/

If you have a minute, I would greatly appreciate your review on amazon's platform to help the book's ranking.

Thank you so much for all your support!

Valerie Sims

Index

A

Aarhus Exhibition of 1909, 70, 72
Administrator's Annual Report 1956, 268
Adverse Possession, 226
Agricultural Exhibition of 1903, 171
Alda, Alan, 300
All Ah We, cobble, 311
Amazon, RMS, 28
America Hill, 53, 173
American Art, Washington DC, 193-4
Anduze, Antoine, 29, 41
Anduze, Rudolph, 115
Anegada, 49-50
Antigua, 114
Apothecary, 40
Arrow, sloop, 144
Arsenic, 40
Aydlett, CC & wife Augusta, 157

B

Bach, Richard, 289, 293-4, 332
Bahamas, 215
Ballenger, Mary Alice, 106, 334
Balsam Hill, 224
Bananas, 29, 53-5, 173, 223, 327
Basketry, 243
Baskets, 71, 173, 223
Bastian, Charles, 128, 188
Bay Leaf, 87, 92, 94, 135, 142-3, 146
Bay Rum, 53, 55, 72, 90-6, 115
Bayberry, 90
Benjamin, Rudolf, 115
Berenjena, 104
Beretta, Dante, 99, 136, 187, 334
Berne, Emile. 122
Bible, 102-103
Biel, Felix, 115
Biggs, Wayne, 213
Billy Bones Beach Bar, 311
Bishop Cory, 268
Blackwood, William, 192
Blake, Cyril, 115
Blake Idalia, 115
Blue Runner, 216
Blue Team, 126
Blyden, Arabella, 327
Booby Birds, 213-14, 238
Booby Rock, 261
Boreham, Donald, 125
Bornn, Gustave, 325-6
Bornn, Victor D., 126
Boulon, Rafe H, 263
Bowden College, 61
Bradley and Francois Insurance, 281n

Brennan, Joe, 291-2
British Consul, 207
Brooks, Mel, 300
Bru Anansi, 239
Bru Takoma, 239
Burk, Charles, 85
Butler, Agnes and John, 263
Bryant, Harold Dr., 241

C

Calabash, 71
Calabash Boom, 289-290
Callwood, Godwin, 308-9
Callwood, Sherman, 301
Canadia, steamer, 94
Caneel Bay, 56, 194-6, 249, 251, 255, 258, 264, 274, 300-315, 331
Carapacho, 211
Caribbean Coal and Fuel Company, 224
Carney, Leslie, 279-280, 283, 290, 292-3, 334
Carney, Richard Joseph, 279-283
Carnival Committee, 145, 176
Carnot, Sadi, Pres., 44-5
Carvel Rock, 261
Cassava, 53, 55, 174-5, 224
Cassi Hill, 285, 286
Castenskiold, Count Henrik Grevenkop, 63, 65-70, 73, 75-76, 82-3, 82
Catherine, S/S, 123
Cattle 20, 37-8, 44, 64, 69, 87, 89, 115, 128, 144, 146, 172, 189-191, 286, 333
CCC Camp, 246
Centerline Road, 243
Central Ironmongery, 51-57, 61
Chapman, Joan, 301
Charlotte Amalie High School, 287
Cheerio, sloop, 136-138
Chevrolet Dealership, 265
China, Blue Cornflower, 107
Chips, motorboat, 192, 195, 220, 223, 233-5
Cholera, 17, 28-9
Christensen, V.A. Dr, 126
Christianity, 102
Christiansted, 7, 28, 136
Christmas, 94, 110, 228-9, 255, 301
Church, Danish Lutheran, 50, 268
Church, Dutch Reformed, 174
Cid, Manuel V., 101, 110
Cinnamon Bay, 17, 49, 42-4, 94, 110, 174, 220
Citric Acid, 86
Civil Works Administration, 242
Clen, Henry, 45
Clen, Lottie, 71, 174
Clyne, Denzel, 302
Coal pot, 216, 220
Cocoa, 35, 53, 71, 105
Coconut, 53, 78, 87, 156, 175, 259
Collins, George L., 246

Columbus, Christopher, vii, 3, 252
Community Motors, 265
Conch stew, 214
Condemnation, 261-2
Condor, motorboat, 195
Conger eel, 200
Congo Bay, 261
Congo Cay, 311-312
Connor, Laurinda, 301
Conservation Service, 154-5
Contributions, 27, 52, 157, 175, 334
Coolidge, Calvin, Pres., 116
Copenhagen, 68, 71, 73, 82, 334
Corneiro, F.M, 122
Costa Rica, 293, 295
Cotton, Sea Island, 32, 53-5, 69, 70, 271
Council Member, 16, 67
Cow Cakes, 131
Cox, Leonard, 263
Crabs, 198, 206, 211-213
Cramer, Lawrence, Gov., 246
Creque, Frank, 138, 186, 198, 205-6, 234
Creque, Marine Railway, 61, 63, 97-8, 137-8, 145, 184, 193, 196, 203, 221, 235
Creque, Cleone, 262
Creque, Emily, 60, 88, 101-110, 138, 148, 151-3, 157, 161, 163-65, 181-2, 192, 198, 201, 228, 234, 249, 254-55, 258, 260-1, 264, 266, 270, 272, 274, 322, 324-25, 331, 334
Creque, Henry O. Jr.,164, 194, 196, 198, 207, 208-11, 221-2, 226, 240, 255, 258, 265-6, 315, 324, 334
Creque, Henry, BVI, 304
Creque, Henry Osmond, 48-50, 53-58, 61, 172, 224, 334
Creque, Henry Owen, 195, 334
Creque, Herman Ogilvie, 39, 49-52. 72. 76-79, 86, 88, 90, 99, 107-8, 110-11, 113-15, 120-127, 129-136, 149, 151, 153, 158, 168, 170-1, 174, 176-79, 180-3, 185-6, 195, 204-7, 211-14, 216-17, 221-2, 246, 306-13,
Creque, John Bedford, 50
Creque, Margaret (Peggy), 257, 264-6, 333
Creque, Margie, 101, 109, 138, 197, 203
Creque, Olga, 164, 198, 203, 228-231, 254, 324
Creque, Valerie, 187-91, 193, 216-17, 241, 254, 258-9, 262-268, 271
Creque's Alley, 265
Creque's Hardware Store, 119, 145
Crevalle Jacks, 220-22
Cricket Association, 145, 176, 188
Cummin, Arch W., 328
Curious Case of Benjamin Button, 102

D

Dalmida, Jimmy, 301
Daniel, Carolina, 115
Danish National Exhibition of 1909, 70
Danish Royal Commissioners, 65
Davis, Arthur, 67
De Castro, Morris Fidanque, 247
De La Rochefoucauld, Francois, 13
De Lagarde, Alberic, 9
De Lagarde, Aimee, 1-6, 37-39, 45, 334
De Lagarde, Caroline, 9
De Lagarde, Count, 3-4
De Lagarde, Dante, 207-9
De Lagarde, Eleonor, 9
De Lagarde, Louis Eugene, 2 9-30, 36-44, 50, 78, 321
De Lagarde, Excelman, 37
De Lagarde, Francois, 37
De Lagarde, G. Sylvanie, 43
De Lagarde, Harry, 2
De Lagarde, John R., 43
De Lagarde, Joseph M. Poniatowsky, 43
De Lagarde, Juste, 9
De Lagarde, Maria Dolores, 50
De Lagarde, Romain, 6-9, 43
De Lamartine, Alphonse, 13
De Musset, Alfred, 13
Deeds, 151, 154, 254, 257, 264-5, 281, 324, 326, 330-1
Deer, White Tail, 209-210
Delinois, Louis, 53, 71
Denmark, Aarhus, 70
Dept. of Public Works, 125, 142
Diary, Blue, 145, 185, 188-9
Dominican Republic, 124, 168, 169
Doves, Zenaida, 209, 211, 211, 239, 241
Drum, Esther (Tootie), 45, 334
Duke & Duchess of Kent, 145

E

Edison, Arthur I., 141
Eloi, Emil, 172
Emancipation, 13, 163
Emmaus, 62, 111
England, 61, 70, 190
Enos, Margaret, 302
Epstein, Jeffrey, 328
Epilepsy, 69
Estate Abrams Fancy, 12, 29, 45
Estate Adrian, 163, 264
Estate Annaberg, 12, 29, 36, 41, 44, 138, 170, 180-1, 238, 244, 249, 254, 259, 264, 318, 326-8
Estate Bakkero, 60, 151
Estate Bordeaux, 60, 66, 71, 77-8, 87, 89, 98-9, 132, 134-6, 151, 153, 244, 295, 325
Estate Brown Bay, 263
Estate Cabritte Horn, 60, 66, 128, 151, 325

Estate Calabash Boom, 289-290
Estate Carolina, 25, 74, 99, 115
Estate Catherineberg, Aka Herman's Farm, 264
Estate Concordia, 60, 249, 254, 260, 264, 325-7
Estate Contant Enighed, 271, 286, 288, 337
Estate Haulover, 62, 264, 324
Estate Hawksnest, 54, 173
Estate Hermitage, 115, 190, 263
Estate Hope, 60, 66, 151, 324
Estate Lamesure 60-330
Estate Leinster Bay, 12-3, 29, 36-8, 41, 44, 71, 78, 215, 238, 264
Estate Lime Tree Bay, 62, 324
Estate Little Plantation, 111
Estate Maho Bay, 54, 327-8
Estate Mandahl, 115
Estate Mary's Point
Estate Misgunst, 60, 66, 151, 325
Estate Mullendal, 264
Estate Parforce, 60, 64, 66, 151, 325
Estate Pearl, 66
Estate Rams Head, 264
Estate Reef Bay, 64, 112, 150, 152, 165, 264, 333
Estate Rendezvous & Ditliff, 331
Estate Rustenberg, 35
Estate Susannaberg, 35, 71, 264
Estate Trunk Bay, 78, 263 268
Estate Turner's Pont, 269
Estate Tutu, 285
Eudora Kean High School, 287
Europe, 61, 69
Evans, Lieutenant, 85
Evans, Waldo, Gov., 122

F

Fabio, Desmond, 208
Fame, sloop, 168, 169
Fancy lacework, 71
Farnsworth, John, Chef, 301
Faulk, Frank R., 150, 152, 264
Fechtenburg, J.H., 176
Fire, 24, 27-8, 85, 97, 99
Firearms, 41, 262
Fish pots, 72, 216, 262
Fishermen, 79, 226
Fishing, 87, 139-40, 155, 187, 192, 196, 201, 204, 207, 216-7, 223, 227, 246, 310, 314, 319
Flamboyant Tree, 161, 219, 240
Folklore Tales, 239
Fort Christian, 15 126
Foster, Edw. B. Rev, 174
France, 3, 5, 8-9, 44, 81
Francis, George, 169
Francis, Carl E., 113, 168, 170, 174, 176, 181, 328
Francis, Lucy, 169
Francois, Cyril V., 126
Fraser, Roslyn, 115
Frenchtown, 110, 184
Fruitcakes, 110
Fuentes, Mike, 214
Fyen, Danish Cruiser, 30, 34

G

Gallows Point, 270, 298
Gates, Margaret Casey, 193-4
Gates, Robert F., 193-4
George, Anika, 103
George, Edward, 329
George, Estelle, 115
George, Eva, 115
George, Franklin, 175
George, Oswald, 63, 324
George, William, 332
Gerard, Mathurine, 42
Gibney, Eleanor, 301, 333
Gilker, Shirley, 216, 334
Glennie, Michael, 303
Goats, 87, 144, 146, 188, 207, 219, 240, 329
Gold Medal, 10, 45, 122
Good Friday, 220
Gordon, Veronica, 281
Govt. House, 17, 243
Grand Hotel, 80
Grass Cay, 262
Great Comet of 1843, 7
Grebe, USS, 99, 115
Grove, David and Barbara, 134, 334
Gutu, 216

H

Haiti, Consul General, 10, 14, 15, 41
Handicrafts, 70, 73, 171
Hang-gliding, 290, 295
Harbor Board, 120, 145, 177
Harbor View Estate, 5
Hardnose fish, 205, 216
Harley, Alphonse, 183, 218
Harley, Joe, 144
Hassel Island, 61, 87, 102, 109, 121, 148, 165, 201, 207, 234
Hedemann, Carl E, 81
Helweg-Larsen, Lars C, 53
Hendricks, Arnold, 112-3
Henley Cay, 311-2
Henri, Grizelda Flori, 37, 42-4
Hoover, Herbert, Pres., 145
Horner, Dave, 159, 334
Horsehair, 39
Horses, 37, 54, 87, 132, 156, 173, 187, 229
Horseshoe Reef, 229
Hough, Governor, 97
Hubler Report, 158, 245
Hubler, Harold, 242, 247
Hugo, Victor, 13
Hunting, 192, 204, 207-212, 216, 219, 240, 262, 308, 319, 328-9
Hurricane Hole, 56
Hurricane Irma of 2017, 78, 314
Hurricane Maria of 2017, 78, 314
Hurricane of 1837, 7

Hurricane of 1867, 18
Hurricane of 1899, 28
Hurricane of 1916, 63, 76, 113, 116
Hurricane San Ciriaco, 38, 56
Hyppolite, Florvil, 15

I

India, sloop,112-3
International Fire and Life Safety Codes, 99

J

Jarvis, Antonio J., 3, 14, 332
Jackson Hole Preserve, Inc., 63, 156-7, 168, 253, 257, 263, 326-7
Jackson, Alfred, 115
Jackson, Daniel, 189
Jackson, Fritz, 189
Jackson, Waldemar "Wally", 128, 185, 189
Johannes, Lucien, 185, 189
Johansen, Edy, 280
Johansen, Ellen, 280
John's Folly, 291, 294
Jorgensen, JP, 97, 173, 324-5, 330, 334
Jost van Dyke, 187, 309
Joseph, Carmelita, 115
Juliet, sloop, 57
Jumbie Jay, 310-311
Jumbie Jr., 311

K

Kaplan, Morris, 249
Kayak, 118, 121-3
Krause, T.M., 18-19
Kerosene Lamps, 163, 201, 224, 238
Kingfish, 207, 216-7
Kittery, USS, 83
Kitty Hawk Land Co. Inc., 157
Kitty Hawk Kites, 290
Knight of Dannebrog, 176
Knight, David W. Sr., 30, 41, 44-5, 163, 332, 334
Knud Hansen Memorial Hospital, 279
Konow, Henri, Com., 80

L

Las Once Mil Virgenes, vii
L'Ouverture, Toussaint, 15
LaBeet, Carl V., 53
Lady Cornelius, sloop, 302
LaFontaine, Alexander and Estelle, 224, 226
Lagerstadt, Lieutenant Seth F.H. and Minnie Lagerstadt, 63, 83-4, 86-7, 89, 324
Larsen, Dave, 301
Lawrence, James, 58
Le Duck, 261
LeCuyer, Francis, 219, 334
Led Zeppelin, 300
Lefee, Sebastian, 111
Legion of Honor, 81
Lemons, 29, 66, 69, 173
Levin, Israel, 45, 49-50, 53
Limes, 29, 53, 66, 69, 73-5, 87, 173, 183, 237, 239
Lindbergh, Charles, 118, 145
Lindqvist, John, 35, 53, 74, 79, 174
Little St. James, 148, 328
Little St. Jeffs, 328
Livestock, 30, 37-8, 44-5, 83, 120, 128-130, 144, 148, 153, 172, 179, 187, 188-191, 196
Lobster, 104, 187, 308-9
Lockhart, Herbert E., 126, 171, 180, 190, 263, 326-7
Lockhart, Ronald, 123, 334
Lord Chesterfield, 13-14
Lottery Tickets, 24
Loubet, Emile, Pres. of France, 81
Lovango Cay, 187, 218, 302, 327

M

MacDonald, Dr., 265
Malacarne, Bob, 159, 295, 334
Magens Bay, 74, 213
Magens, Dr., 25, 26
Magnus, Mabee and Reynard, Inc., 86
Malacarne, Marlene, 2, 223, 228, 241, 269, 271, 274, 285-6, 292, 322, 334
Manneck, Holly, 301
Manta Ray, 311-2
Market Day, Tortola, 222
Marks, Morris A. and wife, Veronique, 157
Marion, USCG, 207, 210
Marsh, William H., 63-5, 74, 175
Martinique, 17, 27-8, 81
Mary's Creek, 136, 199, 206, 224, 236
Matthias, Adalia, 115
Matthias, Alfred, 115
Matthias, Cornelius, 302
Matthias, James Jr., 115
Matthias, James, Sr., 115
Matthias, Mary, 115
Matthias, Winfred, 115
Matta, L.C., 188
Mawson, Alana Lee, 268-9, 290, 334
Mawson, Diane, 62, 106, 166, 214, 235, 241, 268-9, 286, 301, 322, 334
Mawson, Leon A., 211, 260, 287
Mazzini, 14
McDonald, Henry D., 174
Meachum, Tuck, 292
Mexico, 65, 82
Meyers, Sanford
Meyers, Thelma Eliza, Tardy, 102-3, 105, 109-10, 164, 183, 212-221, 235, 237, 239, 266, 272
Michael Cyril E., 254
Mietzefield, Mr., 82
Miller, Marion, 104-5, 204, 229, 235, 241, 266, 270, 286
Miller, Michael, 269
Miller, Richard, 105, 213,

218, 270.
Mingo Cay, 148, 219, 327
Miss Lucy's Restaurant, 326
Moorehead, Theovald E., 262
Moron, Mr., 99, 136
Mourier, I.C., 162-163
Mules, 87, 89, 172, 199
Muller, John, 53

N

National Archives at College Park, 41, 63, 334
National Prohibition Act, 90
Naval Bakery, 102
Needlework, 71
New York, 62, 82, 83, 86, 118, 123, 175, 249, 257, 329, 331
Norman Island, 51, 87, 111, 112, 224, 225, 312

O

O'Neal, Benjamin, 112-3
O'Neal, Ralph, 304
Onions, 51, 53-5, 213, 215, 217
Osborn Clide Eugene, 330-1
Osborn, Clide, Jr., 331

P

Palace Hotel, PR, 228
Palmer, Dr, 115
Pan American Goodwill Flyers, 145
Panama hats, 32
Parade, 122-3
Paramatta, Royal British Mail steamer, 49
Payne, Helen, 271
Pearl, Sloop, 56
Pearson, Paul Martin, Governor, 132, 134, 242-244, 334
Pedophile Island, 328
Pelican Cay, 143
Penn, Izza, 71, 175
Perkins House, 271
Peter Island, 225, 227
Petroglyphs, 112, 165
Pettigrew, Officer, 83, 142
Peyredieu, Jean, 8
Phillips J.D. Motor tugboat, 137-8
Physician, Communal, 25-6
Piano Baby, 106
Picket boats, 193
Pigeon peas, 53
Pigeons, Scaly-Naped, 212
Pillsbury Sound, 219, 328
Pimenta Acris, 90
Pineapples, 29, 53, 55, 174, 224
Pink Pearls, 216
Plant, Roger, 301
Plantain Farm, 170
Poe, Edmund S. Commodore, 51-2
Poems by Valerie Creque-Mawson, 146, 205, 230, 256, 267, 273, 323
Poisoning, 39
Port-au-Prince, 15
Portugal, Lisbon, 119
Potatoes, 51, 55, 171, 174, 215, 220, 224, 269
Pots, Planter 53-5, 165-6
Presley, Priscilla, 301
Prince Carl, HRH, 30-36
Prince, John, 128
Puerto Rico, 56, 80, 85, 123-4, 136-7, 228-9

Q

Queens College, 102
Queen Trigger Fish, 217

R

Reagan, Ronald, Governor, 279
Red Poll Bulls, 189
Redhook, 192, 200, 328
Richards, Halvar Neptune, 263
Riise, A.H., 53, 72, 91-2, 96, 172
Roberts, Alphonso, 112
Rockefeller, Laurance, 157-8, 245, 247-249, 251-258-9, 260, 264, 319
Romer, Franz, 117-118 120, 122-125, 164
Romney, Cyril, 303
Ronalds, Francis Dr., 246
Roosevelt Theodore, Jr. Acting Navy Sec., 116
Rossie Iron Ore Company, 82
Ruhl, Arthur, vii
Rutherford J.T. Congressman, 261-2

S

Saints Peter and Paul Catholic Church, 105, 183, 286
Saunders Gut, 111-112
Schoonover, Bruce and Sharon, 150, 156-7, 247, 332, 334
Scotch Bonnet peppers, 212, 219
Scuba Diving, 307-13
Sea Bird, sloop, 37
Sea Fox, yacht, 174
Seagull, Johnathan Livingston, 289, 294, 332
Second Schleswig War, 16
Selby, Charles C., 288, 290-295, 334
Selby, Mike, 290
Selby, Scott, 290
Selby, Susie, 290
Senepol Cattle, 190
Senegal, 189
Sewer Family, 268
Shadow I, motorboat, 331
Shark, 121, 200, 330-1
Shark Wharf, 200
Shinn, James T., 91
Shinners, Bob, 307
Shipwreck Restaurant, 291
Siddhartha, 102
Simmons, George, 270
Singing Club, 176
Slave Rocks, 234
Slavery, 13, 14, 22
Smith, Alice, 218, 327
Smith, Charlie, 144

Smith, Fritz Allan, 148, 323, 325-6
Smith, James, 209
Smoked Oyster Pie, 104
Spirit of St. Louis, 118
Sprauve, Gerhardt, 263
Sprauve, Julius, 263
Sprauve, Lewis, 112-3
St. Anne's Catholic Church, 183
St. Croix Avis, 19, 52
St. Croix Labor Riot – 1878, 28, 110
St. Croix Rifle Club, 207-8, 210-1
St. Jan Heritage Collective, 320
St. John, M/V, 193
St. John Rescue, Inc., 295
St. Johns Fragrance Company, 95
St. Kitts, 53, 90, 114
St. Lucia, 75
St. Martin, 43
St. Thomae Tidende, 8, 13, 29
St. Thomas Boating Club, 176
St. Thomas New CC team, 179
St. Thomas Rifle Club, 208-9, 211
St. Thomas-St. John Plantation Co., 48, 52, 55, 70
Stakemann, Estella, 177-8, 326
Stakemann, Johan A., 176
Stakemann, Luther, 72, 83, 168, 175-178
StarVilla Vacation Homes, 287, 295, 317, 336
Sterling, Jo, 301
Steven's Cay, 30
Stick, Frank and David, 63, 149-151, 153, 155-7, 248-250, 254, 259, 260, 264, 326, 328, 334
Stick, Maud H., 157
Stokes, Phelps Anson, 174, 333
Submarine Chaser, SC 340, 97, 98
Sugarcane, 69
Suit, Scott, 291, 294
Sullivan, Edwin, Capt. 302
Survey, 42, 99, 100, 125, 136, 152, 154, 156, 242, 328

T

Testamark, Edwin, 99
Testamark, John, 115
Thimbleby, steamer, 94
Thomas, Nathaniel, 128
Thorsen, J.P., 53
Titley, Ethelfreida, 224
Tobacco, 58
Tortola, 40, 58, 64, 69, 114, 167, 222, 223, 333
Tortola Exp. Station, 69
Travers, James Bruce, 307-310
Treasure Island, 224
Trinidad, 73, 102, 174
Truck Farming, 260
Turtle Bay Restaurant, 273, 302, 307

U

Udall, Stewart, 261
Union Hotel, 7
US Soil Conservation Service, 154-155

V

Vagrant Law, 25
Valkyrien, HMS, 77, 80-1
van Beverhoudt, Arnold, 288, 296, 318, 337
van Beverhoudt, Jackie Rose, 228, 235, 241, 285
van Beverhoudt, Joan, 229, 235, 241, 285
van Beverhoudt, Marion, See Miller, Marion
Velveteen Rabbit, 102
Venison, 104, 238
VI Engineering and Survey, 291
Vigilant, Schooner, 68
Viking, Schooner, 68
Vindictive, Sloop, 144
Virgin Gorda, 51, 58
Virgin Islands Daily News, 94, 127, 228, 249, 250-2, 256-7, 260-2, 330, 334
Virgin Islands National Park, 63, 149,158-9, 168, 182, 211, 241-249, 251, 256-7, 260-3, 273, 319, 324-5, 332
Von Scholten, Peter Carl Frederik, 14

W

Walker, Ronald R., 299, 300, 304-5, 321, 334
Walters, Jack, 291
Watson, R. Mr., 242
Wells, Ernest, 115
Wells, Wilfred, 115
West India, Sloop, 112-3
West Indies Training Squadron, 51
Westbrook, Charles Seymour, 63, 82-3, 86
Whistling Cay, 167, 261
White Wings, sailboat, 78
White, Alfred, 67, 70, 73-6, 78-9
White, Alice Penn, 67, 72, 75, 76
Williams, Phillip, Governor, 115
Willie, Captain, 56-7
Willis-Campbell Act, 90
Wilshire, Lancy, 115, 128
Wirth, Conrad, 244, 249
Witty, Arthur, 273
Works Progress Administration, 193
Wright George, M., 241

X

Y

Yams, 55, 173, 223
Yellow Jacks, 216
Yellowtail Snapper, 141, 216, 309

Z

Zabriskie, Luther K., 77, 333

If history were taught in the form of stories

IT WOULD NEVER BE FORGOTTEN

~ Rudyard Kipling

CPSIA information can be obtained
at www.ICGtesting.com
Printed in the USA
LVHW081451090220
646320LV00005B/97